SPICY FAT-FREE
COOKING SECRETS

SPICY FAT-FREE COOKING SECRETS

Over 125 Delicious Recipes Without All the Fat

GITA CHANDRA

PRIMA PUBLISHING

PRIMA PUBLISHING and colophon are registered trademarks of Prima Communications, Inc.

On the cover: *Deviled Eggs with Tofu-Herb Filling (page 110), Mixed Sprout Salad (page 54), Spicy "Stir-Fried" Potatoes (page 186), and Spanish-Style Chicken with Peppers (page 86).*

Library of Congress Cataloging-in-Publication Data

Chandra, Gita.
    Spicy fat-free cooking secrets: over 125 delicious recipes without all the fat / Gita Chandra.
      p. cm.
  Includes index.
  ISBN 0-7615-0547-4
  1. Cookery, International   2. Lowfat diet—Recipes.   3. Spices.
I. Title.
TX725.A1C5136   1997
641.5′ 638—dc21   96-51111
                                                       CIP

97 98 99 00 01 HH 10 9 8 7 6 5 4 3 2 1
Printed in the United States of America

A Note on Nutritional Data
If a range is given for an ingredient amount, the analysis is based on the smaller number. If a range is given for the serving size, the breakdown is based on the larger number. If a choice of ingredients is given in an ingredient listing, the analysis is calculated using the first choice. "Optional" ingredients or those for which no specific amount is stated are not included in the breakdown. Nutritional content may vary depending on the specific brands or types of ingredients used.

How to Order
Single copies may be ordered from Prima Publishing, P.O. Box 1260BK, Rocklin, CA 95677; telephone (916) 632-4400. Quantity discounts are also available. On your letterhead, include information concerning the intended use of the books and the number of books you wish to purchase.

Visit us online at http://www.primapublishing.com

CONTENTS

INTRODUCTION

*S*PICY *FAT-FREE COOKING SECRETS* is the first cookbook to offer a choice of popular cusines from around the world, all prepared without the addition of any fat in the cooking process. This book is proof that delicious food can be made with ease the fat-free way. This concept of cooking is based on five criteria to suit today's fast-paced lifestyle: the food must be delicious, fat free, healthy, global, and fuss free.

This book will be an invaluable aid—in deciding what to eat every day and how to prepare it—for the person serious about weight loss, the health-conscious individual, and the gourmet cook. This style of cooking is ideal for those who must reduce their cholesterol intake but hate boring, dull menus. It is useful for those who love vegetables and are looking for new ways to prepare them. For my vegetarian friends, the vegetarian recipes are *pure* vegetarian (no addition of eggs and animal stock, in any form, in these preparations) and they are truly delicious. To actually enjoy eating and experience a dramatic difference in the way you look and feel without deprivation are reasons enough to try these recipes.

The focus of this book is on dry-roasted spices and fresh herbs, which replace the fat during cooking. This technique puts you in control of how much or how little fat you wish to consume and also how much or how little spice you wish to add to the food. The recipes are very select, and the essence of this book is to impart a gourmet cooking skill. Once mastered (which is very easy to do), this technique can be used to create any recipe. Spices roasted at very high heat emit wonderful flavors, which give natural taste to the marvelous recipes in this book. Fresh herbs blend well with the spices and add their own unique aroma. The possibilities for substituting spices and interchanging herbs to suit individual tastes are endless.

Spicy Fat-Free Cooking Secrets is a book for everyone. Every medical expert cautions against the consumption of excess fat, salt, sugar, and processed foods. According to them, enough fat already exists in the food we eat, and no more needs to be added. Unfortunately, the average American consumes at least eight times the fat that the body needs, reports Dr. Dean Ornish, a world-renowned physician, in his bestseller, *Program for Reversing Heart Disease* (Ballantine, 1991). Medical experts have also recommended that we cut back on our meat consumption and make lowfat vegetarian foods the bulk of our diet; therefore, the fish and chicken servings in this book are smaller than the vegetarian servings. Fortunately, no one has as yet placed a restriction on the use of natural spices and herbs—and there we have the answer to great fat-free cooking.

The spices used in the following recipes are in all likelihood already in your spice rack, because you probably use them all the time and they are easily available in the local supermarket. What makes these recipes special is the different combinations of these very spices, along with a simple step-by-step approach and, above all, very quick cooking. The recipes are appetizing and the process is quick, creating meals that are superb, fast, and fat free and that automatically eliminate a considerable percentage of your daily fat intake without compromising on taste. You can throw out all your curry powder, which isn't an authentic representative of any ethnic cuisine, and don't waste your money buying any more exotic sauces, instant mixes, and salt-laden processed food to appease your craving for taste. And cleanup is easy, not greasy.

Using this cookbook, you can plan a lavish dinner party, and your guests will never believe the entire menu is fat free! You may eat food that is prepared without fat all week or one day a week. Whether you are entertaining or cooking for yourself, whether you try just one dish or make an entire meal the fat-free way, this book will change your whole perspective about cooking and eating. Your guests will love you for it, and your family will be grateful that you won't be feeding them the excess fat that will stay with them for the rest of their lives.

THE ORIGINS AND CURATIVE PROPERTIES OF COMMONLY USED HERBS AND SPICES

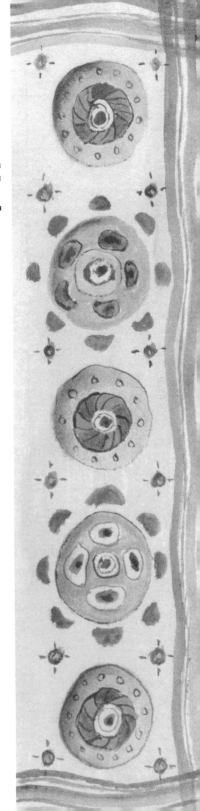

Spices, the natural flavoring agents added to food, are made from the dried seeds, fruit, flowers, and leaves of herbs. An herb is a plant whose leaves, stems, roots, flowers, or fruit have culinary or medicinal uses. In the ancient civilizations of India, Egypt, China, Greece, and Rome, many herbs were known to have medicinal powers and were used in the treatment of chronic diseases. They were added to food in specific proportions to aid in digestion, provide taste, and help cure common ailments. Modern researchers in the field of pharmacology and cosmetology are just beginning to grasp the curative powers of the more than 1,000 plant species that are described in early Indian and Chinese literature.

Spices were as highly valued as gold and silver in the early times and were an important trade item. They still play a dominating role as an item of export in the Far East. The Romans brought back exotic spices from India in the first century and introduced the West to an array of new flavors, which were used in perfumes and food. Explorers including Vasco da Gama are credited with introducing Europe to the spices from the East. Christopher Columbus changed the way the world cooks by bringing to Europe the culinary traditions of South and Central America. Such was the importance of spices that wars took place to gain control over the growing spice colonies.

Until the Middle Ages, spices were only consumed in Europe in the palaces of aristocrats, while the common people basically ate boiled, bland food topped with mustard (the only affordable spice). On the other hand, the bustling markets of India and China were teeming with spice vendors, and spicy food was a way of life for the rich and poor alike. Today, along with conventional drugs, the use of spices and herbal medication for the treatment of chronic ailments is common in the Far East and is gaining acceptance in the West.

From the health point of view, the technique of adding the right blend of roasted spices can go a long way in reducing the amount of salt, fat, and sugar added for flavor. If you love flavorful cuisine, herbs and spices are the answer. Your only guide should be your taste, so experimentation is definitely the key.

This section will discuss only those herbs that are ingredients in the recipes in this book and that are believed to have medicinal properties. Under no circumstances should anyone use an herb as a substitute for professional medical advice in the treatment of a disease or disorder. For suggestions on where to buy spices in bulk or how to extend the life of herbs and spices see "Useful Tips and Time-Saving Techniques."

Black Pepper

The terms black pepper and peppercorn evolved from the Sanskrit word *pippali*, which means berry.

These small berries are picked green and are dried in the sun until they blacken and shrink. Black pepper was coveted like gold and dominated the spice trade. Culinary history indicates that Romans seasoned their food heavily with this spice, which they obtained from the western coast of India. Later, the Arabs were fascinated by black pepper and sought to establish trade routes to the East. Malaysia and Brazil are the major producers of pepper today. Ground black pepper is considered beneficial for the common cold, amnesia, muscular pains, and indigestion.

Cardamom

The third most expensive spice in the world after saffron and vanilla, cardamom is one of the most aromatic and natural flavoring agents to use in poultry, fish, and vegetable dishes. India is the largest producer of the cardamom plant, followed by Sri Lanka and Guatemala. Ground cardamom is made from the seeds of the ginger family, which grows in the rain forests of India. It was recognized for its therapeutic properties as far back as 1000 A.D., when it was brought to Europe by the Portuguese, Greeks, and Romans. They used cardamom in perfumes and also as a breath freshener. In Germany, Russia, and Scandinavia, this aromatic spice is used to flavor cakes and pastries. In India, ground cardamom mixed with ginger, cloves, and coriander is believed to be a digestive aid, which is why cardamom tea is served at the end of a sumptuous meal. Ground cardamom should be purchased in small amounts and stored in airtight containers.

Chili Pepper or Cayenne

This hot condiment is available in its dried red, hot form or as the fresh green chili pepper, which belongs to the capsicum family. Cayenne is made by grinding a variety of the dried red, hot pepper to a fine powder. Archeological research indicates that for thousands of years a variety of chili peppers was cultivated in the valleys of Mexico. It was here that Columbus first observed the peppers being consumed in vast quantities by the natives. They are an integral part of Mexican, Indian, Thai, and Chinese cuisine because of their fiery taste. The superb cuisine of the southwestern United States owes much to the flavor of fresh green peppers. In Europe and the rest of the U.S., they are used in the preparation of hot sauce and Tabasco sauce. In terms of sheer volume, chili peppers are the largest grown spice in any part of the world. There are over 200 different types of chilies, and India, Mexico, China, and Indonesia are the largest producers. They are rich in vitamin C and were also used in ancient times to prepare an ointment to relieve aching muscles and joints. Medical experts today believe that chili peppers act as a decongestant to relieve cold symptoms. From the culinary aspect, they add color as well as "heat" to the food.

Gradual addition in food, depending on one's tolerance level, is a wise idea.

Cilantro (Chinese Parsley)

Cilantro or Chinese parsley resembles regular parsley in its bright green color and the shape of its leaves. However, this herb has a distinct flavor and is extensively used for taste as well as garnish. It is native to the cuisines of India, Mexico, Thailand, and southern Europe. It is the main ingredient for various chutneys, dips, and relishes. If this herb is not available, chopped parsley and chopped fresh chives in equal ratio may be substituted in some dishes. Whenever a recipe calls for chopped cilantro, the reference is to the cilantro leaves and small stems; the large stems should be discarded. The leaves should be washed and drained before use.

Cinnamon

Cinnamon was known to ancient physicians before 2700 B.C. Indians knew about its therapeutic value in the eighth century. The oldest recorded description of cinnamon is given in the Torah; mention of it is also made in the Bible and in Sanskrit literature. Indian and Middle Eastern cooking requires the addition of cinnamon in meat and poultry, while in the West it is mainly limited to desserts. Cinnamon was used in many cultures as a remedy for asthma, paralysis, digestive disorders, and the common cold. Ground cinnamon should be purchased in small quantities and stored tightly sealed to retain its aroma. In this book, this ingredient is mostly used in its ground form.

Clove

This spice is actually a flower bud from the clove tree, which originated in Moluccas, popularly known as the Spice Islands, in Southeast Asia. Clove has been used in India and China for more than 2,000 years. It is believed that the Chinese came to learn about it in the third century B.C. Subsequently, clove was traded throughout Europe from Asia. At present, Zanzibar is the leading producer of clove, followed by Malaysia and Sri Lanka. Clove was known to have many medicinal properties. It was used to prevent tooth decay and to relieve toothaches, bad breath, cough, and earache. Whole cloves can be ground in an electric grinder, or small quantities of ground cloves can be purchased. Ground clove is more potent than whole clove, and only a pinch of it is required in a recipe.

Coriander Seeds

The yellowish brown seeds that are plucked and dried from the coriander or cilantro herb is ground to make coriander. There are the Moroccan and Indian varieties, and both are extensively grown in Europe, north Africa, India, Iran, Central and South America, and Asia. They have a pleasantly spicy taste and were used for their medicinal value for 3,000 years. Coriander has been around for a long time— coriander seeds were discovered in the tombs of Egyptian pharaohs. Ground coriander is said to relieve acidity, cure migraine, lower cholesterol, and remedy certain skin disorders. It is an essential ingredient in Thai and Indian cuisine. In the West it is used to flavor certain alcoholic beverages.

Cumin Seeds

This aromatic dried seed is derived from an herbaceous plant found in the eastern Mediterranean region, Syria, Turkey, India, and Arabia. It was a well-known spice in the Middle Ages, used to spice ground meat and poultry. Cumin is believed to have originated in the Nile Valley of Egypt and its use spread quickly due to the caravan trade. Cumin is known to relieve digestive disorders, insomnia, cold symptoms, and scorpion stings. Whole seeds can be ground in a coffee or spice grinder. Both whole and ground cumin are used in the recipes in this book.

Dill

This tall, graceful herb is native to the Mediterranean region, southern Russia, and Scandinavia. Its rich green, feathery leaves and biting flavor make it a popular flavoring agent. It has been used for thousands of years for its medicinal and culinary properties. During the Middle Ages, it was used as a protection against witchcraft in the countries of central Europe, Scandinavia, and Germany. Greeks covered their heads with dill leaves to encourage restful sleep. Dill was also believed to aid in respiratory ailments, digestive disorders, bad breath, and swelling of the joints. Dill leaves, boiled in water, were consumed to stop hiccups.

Fennel

By the eighth century, fennel was used throughout Europe. Before the eighth century, it was known in ancient India, China, and Egypt. Fennel is a tall, hardy perennial of the parsley family with small, ridged oval seeds. Its use was spread by the Romans, from India and China to Europe. There are legendary tales from the thirteenth century of its aphrodisiac qualities. "Fennel seeds drunk with wine stirreth lechery" was a popular belief of the Romans. Commonly cultivated in many countries, fennel is a popular ingredient, both as a vegetable and a spice. It was considered a safe household remedy for colic in babies. Inhaling the steam from boiled fennel leaves is believed to aid in respiratory disorders. The seeds taste like anise and are chewed as a breath freshener. They are regarded as a cure for flatulence and are supposed to be good for the eyes.

Garlic

Garlic is among the most ancient herbs of the onion family and has been highly valued for centuries. Khnoum Khoufuf, the builder of the oldest pyramid in 4500 B.C., valued garlic to such an extent that he ordered his builders to consume it daily. Hippocrates, the Greek physician who lived from 460 B.C. to 357 B.C., encouraged the consumption of garlic to prevent infectious diseases. The Chinese have used garlic since 3000 B.C. and it is the most important ingredient in their cuisine. Garlic is considered a magical herb by today's medical experts. Studies have shown that consuming one clove of garlic a day reduces cholesterol by 9 percent (*Prevention* magazine, March 1994 issue). Its healing properties go far beyond adding zip to food. It contains chemicals that thin the blood and it is the most natural way to lower cholesterol and prevent arteriosclerosis. Garlic was also used to cure tuberculosis, cancer, diseases of the liver, gall bladder, asthma, cough, and rheumatism. Since this herb is a common ingredient in most recipes, it saves time and labor to peel and puree in a food processor quite a few cloves at one time. The cooking technique of this book requires that garlic be added in its pureed form, which is referred to as "processed garlic" throughout the book.

Ginger

Ginger is said to have its origins in India and was introduced to eastern Asia from very early times. In

Sanskrit scriptures it is called *singabhera*. Later, the Greeks named it *zingibheri*, from which the Latin name *zingiber* came about, which eventually became ginger, as the world knows it today. By the ninth century, use of ginger was common in Europe. The knobby rhizomes were easy to transport and were brought to Africa in the thirteenth century and to the West Indies in the sixteenth century. The medicinal powers of this "natural healer" were described in Vedic literature several thousand years ago. Ginger's most important medicinal value is its ability to settle digestive disorders, colic, flatulence, and sluggish livers. Ginger-flavored hot tea is the common man's cure for a cough or sore throat. The medicinal value of ginger as well as its fresh pungent flavor make it an important ingredient in Oriental and Indian cuisines. It is still widely used as a household remedy in Asian countries.

To use ginger, the light brown skin needs to be peeled and the ginger should then be chopped and processed in a food processor. In its processed form, ginger looks "stringy" because of the threadlike texture of the root. It will keep for a week in the refrigerator. It can also be frozen in airtight containers. Ginger in its pureed form is referred to as "processed ginger" in this book.

Mint

As a culinary herb, the cool refreshing taste of mint makes it a favorite in Far Eastern, Middle Eastern, and Western cuisines. Roast leg of lamb with mint sauce, tabbouleh, yogurt raita spiced with mint, mint tea of north Africa, and mint-flavored liqueurs and desserts are some popular preparations made with this perennial herb. Among the many varieties, the most popular is the bright green garden species called spearmint. Owing to its antibacterial properties, mint is used today in mouthwash, toothpaste, breath fresheners, and dental floss. Contemporary herbal medical experts recommend the use of mint in the treatment of influenza, coughs, and colds. Dried mint is a good substitute for fresh mint and should be stored in a cool place in an airtight container.

Mustard Seeds

Black, white, or brown mustard is the seed of the mustard plant, a member of the cabbage family. The seeds are small and round. *Brassica nigra*, or black mustard seeds, have the most distinctive flavor of all and are used in many recipes in this book. They were liberally added to food by the Romans and Greeks as far back as the fifth century. The Romans called it *sinapis* and in Italian it is *senape*. The word mustard means "to burn" in Latin. White mustard is used in the American prepared mustard sold commercially. The use of mustard seeds and mustard oil was said to result in flawless skin and to encourage hair growth. A massage with warm mustard oil is believed to relieve muscular pain.

Nutmeg

There is no equivalent to this potent spice for aroma and flavor, and very small amounts are used in recipes. It is made by grinding the aromatic seed of the nutmeg tree, which was first discovered in Moluccas (the Spice Islands). It was regularly used in India and China to spice up food and also to aid in digestive disorders. Arabs use it in small quantities in meat preparations. In the West, it is mostly used in desserts. Its healing powers were recognized from early times and it was viewed as a remedy for skin disorder, liver disorder, rheumatism, insomnia, and dehydration. Cultivated in Sri Lanka, Malaysia, Indonesia, and the West Indies, nutmeg is today widely used by pharmaceutical companies in the manufacture of medicines, hair products, soaps, and perfumes.

Onion

The origin of this herb seems to be in the Middle East. It was known as a curative herb in Egypt, where it is pictured on tombs dating as far back as 3200 B.C. Mention of the onion also appears in the Bible. Today, it is cultivated extensively throughout the world. Modern research indicates that onion contains chemical agents that suppress the clotting of blood and lower blood pressure. This chemical is retained in the onion even after it is cooked. Herbal research shows that it was used as a cure for cough, bronchitis, and thrombosis and as a safe preventive medicine against the common cold because of its heat-inducing quality. It was also regarded as a potent aphrodisiac when taken with honey. It is rich in vitamin C.

For the unique style of cooking in this book, the onions must be peeled, chopped, and processed in a food processor. Since onions contain a strong acid that stings the eyes and tastes bitter, many recipes require that peeled and chopped onion should be rinsed in cold water and drained before use. Processed onion should be stored in airtight containers and will last for a week in the refrigerator. It may also be frozen. For a whole week of fat-free cooking using the recipes in this book, five or six large onions should be processed at a time. Two medium onions are the equivalent of five heaping tablespoons of processed onion. Throughout this book, the term "processed onion" refers to peeled, chopped, rinsed, and drained onions that have been pureed in a food processor.

Paprika

This is a mild red powdery condiment derived from ripe, sweet peppers. It provides rich, natural color to the food and, when combined with other spices, gives texture and flavor without the "heat" of cayenne.

Saffron

The most exquisite and the most expensive spice in the world, one pound of saffron requires the harvesting of over a quarter of a million crocus flowers. Fortunately, only four or five threads need to be used at one time. Saffron has been used in cooking for thousands of years. Some chefs will use turmeric as a substitute; this is not recommended, because these spices produce entirely different flavors even though they both emit a yellow color. Spain is the main producer of saffron, though it is also cultivated in some Mediterranean countries. This spice should only be purchased in the thread form to ensure purity and should never be used in excess. It should be stored in a tightly sealed container and will last for years.

Thyme

About 100 species of thyme are believed to exist. Thyme was popular in ancient Greece, where it was used to strengthen the lungs and to cure gout. It has a robust flavor, which makes it an important culinary ingredient in a bouquet garni. It is used extensively in European cuisine. Its subtle flavor enhances the taste of fish, vegetables, and soups. It is a commonly used spice in Italian cooking and is easily available in both fresh and dried forms.

Turmeric

Turmeric adds brilliant color and flavor to food and has been in use for the last 2,000 years in India and

China. The short, fleshy, underground rhizomes belong to the ginger family and are ground to make commercial turmeric powder. Researchers claim that this perennial herb originated in Southeast Asia. During his travels to China, Marco Polo observed its brilliant yellow color and mistook it for saffron. Due to a brisk spice trade in the seventh century, it was carried to the East Indies and transported over the Pacific to Hawaii by the Polynesians. Turmeric is alluded to in early Sanskrit literature as having dominant medicinal qualities. It was accepted as a healing herb in early civilizations. It is well known as a blood purifier and a cure for intestinal disorders. Its antiseptic properties made it an effective remedy for chronic cough and throat irritation. It was also applied to open wounds and burns on the skin. In India today, it is used as a home remedy, a natural dye, and a cosmetic applied to the skin.

USEFUL TIPS AND TIME-SAVING TECHNIQUES

This book aims for great results with no fuss and no wasting of time. Keeping brevity in mind, the concise list below has some useful tips that you might want to read over to make the best use of the recipes that follow.

Processing Ingredients

A food processor is necessary for the preparation of most of the recipes. Certain basic ingredients, such as onion, garlic, and ginger, must be pureed so that they cook in their own juice thereby providing a rich texture and flavor without the use of oil. Since most recipes call for these basic ingredients, ample quantities should be processed at one time. Directions for pureeing these ingredients are in the section "Processed Ginger, Garlic, and Onion." If you do not have a food processor, any kitchen gadget that can puree onion, garlic, and ginger without the addition of water could be used instead.

Chopped or sliced onion should be rinsed in cold water and drained before processing or adding to a recipe so that the strong flavor is somewhat reduced.

Chutney, salsa, and dips can be pureed consecutively without washing the food processor bowl and blade after each use. As a general rule of thumb, vegetables should be processed before meat and fish.

A handheld chopper or blender that purees ingredients directly in the saucepan is convenient, though not essential. Lumps can be eliminated with ease from sauces and soups with this gadget; however, a food processor will work just as well.

Spices: Purchasing, Storing, and Using

The number of spices used in these recipes requires obtaining them at a reasonable cost. Initially, when you begin experimenting with this cooking technique, you can always purchase the ground spices from your local supermarket. Later, you might find that your supermarket has a bulk food section, or you may have a wholesaler or ethnic store in your area that you could visit every few months. Spices and dry herbs could also be ordered by mail from a reliable mail-order company: try Attar Herbs and Spices, 21 Playground Road, New Ipswich, NH 03071; (800) 541-6900 (order placement). You can request a catalog, free of charge, by calling (603) 878-1780. The company requests a minimum order of $50 in one-pound minimum quantities; if this is too much for you, try sharing the order with a friend. Before ordering by mail, it is wise to determine approximately how much of each kind of spice is typically used. Some spices, such as turmeric, cumin, and black pepper, should be ordered in larger quantities than cardamom or cloves, which are used sparingly. You may order whole spices and grind small quantities at a time in an electric coffee or spice grinder, or you can buy them ground. The aroma of freshly ground spices is worth the extra effort, and this method ensures that the spices you buy have no additives.

To help you to identify your spices easily, label your dry spice containers clearly, as some of them, such as ground cumin and ground coriander, may look identical. The method of storing spices for a long period depends to a great extent on where you live. In hot, humid places like Florida, dry spices will not last for very long at room temperature; they must be stored in clearly labeled, airtight containers in the freezer. Take out a month's supply and thaw on the counter, ensuring that no moisture gets in the spices. In the colder climates of the north, store in a cool, dry pantry. Clean, dry spoons should be used to scoop out spices, as moisture will encourage fungus growth.

Investing in lazy Susans that fit inside kitchen cabinets ensures that spices are easily accessible. Label spices clearly, store them in airtight, clear plastic or glass containers, and place them with the label side facing out on the lazy Susans. Spices that are frequently used should be grouped together.

Herbs: Storing and Using

To make expensive herbs last longer, the stem and root should be submerged in a jar or mug of water (as you would fresh flowers). Cover the leaves loosely with a plastic grocery bag to prevent them from drying out and store in the refrigerator. Herbs will last up to ten days as long as the stems are submerged. Pluck as many leaves as you require and leave the rest intact.

Herbs are interchangeable in a recipe, and substitutes work well. Basil in place of cilantro, or fresh dill instead of parsley, will taste interestingly different. It will also save you a trip to the store every time a recipe calls for an herb that may not be on hand.

Cooking Without Fats: Preventing Foods from Burning or Sticking

Since no oil is added during cooking, minced onion or garlic will naturally tend to stick to the pot. To prevent the food from burning, lower the heat and gradually add a tablespoon of tomato puree, tomato juice, water, or nonfat plain yogurt.

Good-quality stainless steel and nonstick pans will achieve the best results. Use large cooking pots and saucepans, because food cooks faster and more evenly when the base area exposed to the heat is larger. A six-quart stainless steel pot to cook two pounds of chicken, for instance, is ideal. Triple-ply, heavy-base stainless steel cookware is perfect, because the thicker the base, the better the results. This does not mean that all standard stainless steel cookware should be discarded. Aluminum and copper utensils are not recommended, as these metals react when they come in contact with acidic substances like lime juice, vinegar, or yogurt. Nonstick cookware is generally used for browning and quick stir-fry dishes and nonstick cooking spray is required in some of the recipes. Spices roasted in nonstick cookware will take a minute or so longer to roast, because the nonstick coating takes more time to heat.

Coating Foods: Lowfat and Efficient Methods

Whenever time permits, process ample quantities of corn flakes and store in an airtight container; use them for coating in place of bread crumbs, which contain fat. A combination of equal parts of whole wheat flour and cornmeal is also a good coating to use.

The most efficient way to coat any item is to put a sheet of paper towel on a plate and spread one or two tablespoons of flour or bread crumbs (or corn flakes) on the paper towel. Put the item on it and gently lift the edges of the paper towel all around. The coating "settles" on and around the item.

Controlling Cooking Times and Temperatures

Temperature control and timing are vital, especially during the roasting of dry spices, which is a quick process. When cooking on an electric stove, remove the pot from the burner whenever you want to stop cooking, because the electric coils remain very hot even when they are turned off (whereas gas burners can be switched off instantly). A useful tip to ensure that spices are roasted just right is to watch for a very slight amount of smoke rising from the pot. Immediately lowering the heat or taking the pot off the heat and adding the next ingredient stops the cooking process and prevents the spices from burning.

Cooking time increases if the quantity of food being cooked increases. Increasing the amount of onion and garlic, for instance, will increase the amount of time it takes for these ingredients to cook in their own juice. Dry spices, on the other hand, do not take much longer to roast, since they are generally increased only by a third.

Turning Foods Without Breaking Them

Using two implements (a spatula and fork, for instance) makes it easier to flip over fritters, cutlets, and patties. It prevents "chasing" the food around the pan. Use one tool to carefully pry the food up and hold it in position, then use the other implement to gently turn the food over without breakage.

Ingredients in a Well-Stocked Pantry

A well-stocked pantry makes recipe planning versatile. Assorted vinegars, such as distilled white, red wine, apple cider, balsamic, and rice vinegar, are used in most recipes from around the world. In addition to all-purpose flour, you can try pastry flour, cornmeal flour, semolina, oat bran, and whole wheat flour; by themselves or in combination with other flours, they form the base ingredient for batter, coating, or browning.

Boiled potatoes are used in a variety of ways in many of the recipes. Save time by boiling a few potatoes each week, as needed, and storing them in the refrigerator. Boiled, unpeeled potatoes will last a week.

Firm or extra-firm lowfat tofu is recommended for all recipes calling for tofu.

Brown sugar is as important an ingredient as regular white sugar.

Lemon juice and lime juice can be substituted for each other in all recipes.

Don't dispose of skim milk just because it is past the expiration date. Make plain or vanilla yogurt, or simply boil it, cool, and store in a clean container in the refrigerator. Skim the "skin" that forms on the surface just before use.

Adapting Old Recipes to Be New Fat-Free Favorites

Recycle old recipes and make them fat free by using some of the techniques in this book. Remember, you control the fat and cholesterol content in the recipe, not the other way around.

PROCESSED GINGER, GARLIC, AND ONION

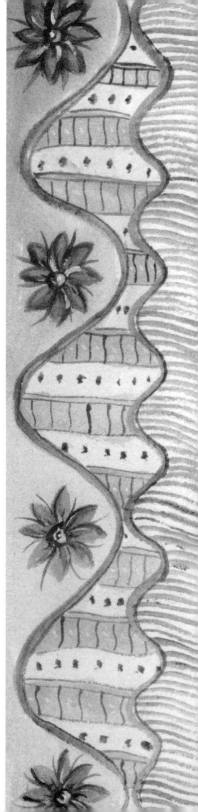

Processing ginger, garlic, and onion is vital to most recipes in this book. In their processed form, these ingredients cook in their own juice, eliminating the need for oil when cooking. If processed in advance, the preparation time for most recipes is significantly reduced. In this book, "processed" ginger, garlic, and onion refers to these ingredients pureed or finely minced in a food processor.

Processed garlic and onion can turn yellow when stored in the refrigerator. This natural change occurs because they release an acid that changes their color; they can be used safely in recipes and will not change the taste or texture. Processed ginger, garlic, and onion may be refrigerated for ten days or frozen for a month. Use the same airtight containers for these ingredients each time they are prepared. When containers are not in use, they should be washed, dried with a paper towel, and closed snugly until ready for use.

PROCESSED GINGER

YIELD: 2½ TABLESPOONS

Processed ginger can be used in place of grated ginger in any recipe.

1 (3½-inch) piece of ginger

Peel and chop the ginger. Place in a food processor fitted with the metal blade.

Puree to a "stringy" consistency. With a spatula, scrape the sides of the bowl frequently during processing.

Place in an airtight container and refrigerate or freeze.

EACH TEASPOON PROVIDES
5 calories, 0.1 g protein, 0.9 g carbohydrate
0 g fat, 1 mg sodium, 0 mg cholesterol

PROCESSED GARLIC

YIELD: 8 TEASPOONS

Due to its texture, processed garlic looks "minced." It can be used in place of minced or pressed garlic.

1 head (approximately 16 cloves) of garlic

Separate the head and peel the garlic cloves.

Place the garlic in the food processor and puree; this takes no more than a few seconds. Scrape the sides of the bowl occasionally, with a spatula, during processing to ensure a uniform "minced" consistency.

Immediately transfer to an airtight container and refrigerate or freeze.

EACH TEASPOON PROVIDES
8 calories, 0.4 g protein, 2.0 g carbohydrate
0 g fat, 2 mg sodium, 0 mg cholesterol

PROCESSED ONION

YIELD: 10 TABLESPOONS

Chopped onion emits a strong acid that stings the eyes. A large bowl of cold water should be kept at hand to soak the chopped onion. This ensures that some of the acid in the onion is rinsed off. Do not process red or white onions; red onions are too strong and white onions are too bland. Onions, when processed, look "pureed" because of their juice.

4 medium yellow onions

Peel and chop the onions. Rinse chopped onion in cold water and drain.

Process the onion to form a puree, scraping the sides of the bowl occasionally with a spatula.

Immediately transfer to an airtight container and refrigerate or freeze.

EACH TABLESPOON PROVIDES
24 calories, 0.7 g protein, 5.2 g carbohydrate
0.1 g fat, 0 mg sodium, 0 mg cholesterol

SOUPS

CREAM OF SPINACH SOUP

YIELD: 4 SERVINGS

This is a good choice at the start of a meal. Although there are many variations to this soup, this is the simplest. The soup may be strained for a smoother texture, but fiber and nutrients will be lost in the process.

1 cup frozen cut or leaf spinach, thawed
¼ cup chopped onion
1 clove garlic
1½ cups water
1½ cups skim milk
Salt and pepper to taste
2 tablespoons cornstarch mixed with
   3 tablespoons skim milk
Dash Tabasco sauce

Process the spinach with the onion, garlic, and as much water as necessary (generally ¼ cup is ample) to form a puree. Place a 3-quart stainless steel saucepan on medium-high heat, add the spinach puree and 1½ cups water, and bring to a boil. Add the milk, salt, and pepper and cook on medium-high heat for 2 minutes. Reduce heat to low. Gradually add the cornstarch mixture and stir until the soup is thickened to desired consistency. Strain if you prefer a smooth texture. Serve hot, topped with Tabasco sauce.

EACH SERVING PROVIDES

70 calories, 5.3 g protein, 12.4 g carbohydrate

0.3 g fat, 98 mg sodium, 2 mg cholesterol

SERVING SUGGESTION

Serve with savory stuffed potatoes (page 188), a garden salad, and garlic toast (page 214).

BRAZILIAN BLACK BEAN SOUP

YIELD: 3 SERVINGS

This rich and savory soup is popular in some countries in Latin America. Clove and cumin are used extensively to add flavor to the cuisine of this region.

2 cups canned black beans, rinsed and drained
2 cups water
½ teaspoon processed garlic
¼ cup diced onion
⅛ teaspoon ground clove
¼ teaspoon ground cumin
1 tablespoon lime juice
1 teaspoon hot sauce, or to taste
Salt to taste
1 finely sliced scallion

Puree half the beans in a food processor or blender, adding a little water if necessary.

Combine the pureed beans, whole beans, water, garlic, onion, clove, cumin, lime juice, hot sauce, and salt in a 4-quart stainless steel pot and bring to a boil. Reduce the heat to low, cover, and simmer for 25 minutes. Adjust seasoning and add additional lime juice, if necessary. Pour into bowls and top with scallion. Serve steaming hot.

EACH SERVING PROVIDES

156 calories, 10.1 g protein, 29.0 g carbohydrate

0.6 g fat, 634 mg sodium, 0 mg cholesterol

SERVING SUGGESTION

Serve with asparagus-mushroom crostini (page 212) and a mixed green salad.

CHINESE HOT AND SOUR SOUP

YIELD: 3 SERVINGS

This soup can be prepared ahead of time and refrigerated. It will last three to four days in the refrigerator. Vegetables such as mushrooms and canned water chestnuts (drained) can replace the green beans and cabbage.

½ teaspoon processed ginger
½ teaspoon processed garlic
½ cup fresh snow peas or fresh green beans, sliced
½ cup finely sliced green cabbage (optional)
½ cup peeled and finely sliced carrots sticks
2 cups water
1 cup extra-firm lowfat tofu, cut in 1-inch squares
3 tablespoons low-sodium soy sauce
3 tablespoons distilled white vinegar
2 tablespoons hot sauce, or to taste
Salt to taste
2 tablespoons arrowroot mixed with
    4 tablespoons water
1 scallion, finely sliced (green ends included)

Place a 4-quart stainless steel pot on medium heat. Add the ginger and garlic and stir for 40 seconds.

Add the snow peas, cabbage, carrots, and water. Bring to a boil on high heat, cover, reduce heat to low, and cook for approximately 5 minutes or until vegetables are crisp-tender.

Add the tofu, soy sauce, vinegar, hot sauce, and salt. Gradually add the arrowroot mixture, stirring continuously to avoid lumps. If the soup gets too thick, add more water to the soup. Adjust seasoning and soy sauce to taste. Add scallion and serve hot.

EACH SERVING PROVIDES
93 calories, 8.3 g protein, 13.6 g carbohydrate
1.2 g fat, 761 mg sodium, 0 mg cholesterol

MINESTRONE SOUP

YIELD: 6 SERVINGS

This soup is a meal in itself. Any combination of vegetables and beans can be used. For a thicker consistency, puree the beans before adding to the soup.

½ teaspoon dried basil
½ teaspoon dried oregano
2 bay leaves
1 cup chopped onion
1 tablespoon processed garlic
1 cup frozen peas and carrots or mixed vegetables
½ cup chopped celery
1 cup chopped fresh or canned tomatoes
½ cup canned tomato puree
½ cup canned chickpeas, rinsed and drained
½ cup canned kidney beans, rinsed and drained
Salt and pepper to taste
2¾ cups water
1 tablespoon lemon juice
4 sprigs chopped parsley

Set a 6-quart stainless steel pot on medium-high heat. Add the basil, oregano, and bay leaves and cook for 1 minute. Add the onion and garlic and cook for 1 minute. Add the peas and carrots, celery, tomatoes, tomato puree, chickpeas, kidney beans, salt, pepper, water, lemon juice, and parsley and bring to a quick boil on high heat. Reduce the heat to low, cover, and simmer for about 30 minutes or until vegetables are just cooked. Discard the bay leaves. Adjust seasoning if necessary. Remove from heat and serve hot.

EACH SERVING PROVIDES
85 calories, 4.1 g protein, 17.5 g carbohydrate
0.6 g fat, 199 mg sodium, 0 mg cholesterol

SERVING SUGGESTION

Serve with garlic toast (page 214) on the side and fruit salad for dessert..

SLIMMERS VEGETABLE SOUP

YIELD: 4 SERVINGS

Here is a soup that can be eaten anytime, and in any quantity, without worrying about calories. You can use any combination of leafy vegetables. Crisp vegetables, such as snow peas and water chestnuts, are especially good.

4 cups tomato juice
2 cups sliced cabbage (any kind)
1 teaspoon processed garlic
2 heaping tablespoons processed onion
1 cup chopped frozen broccoli
1 cup frozen cut green beans
1 cup sliced fresh mushrooms
Salt and pepper to taste
Pinch dried basil
Pinch dried thyme
2 tablespoons distilled white vinegar
Dash Tabasco sauce or hot sauce

Put all ingredients in a 6-quart stainless steel pot, cover, and bring to a boil on high heat. Reduce heat to low and simmer for 10 minutes or until vegetables are crisp-tender. Serve hot.

EACH SERVING PROVIDES
92 calories, 5.0 g protein, 21.3 g carbohydrate
0.5 g fat, 903 mg sodium, 0 mg cholesterol

SERVING SUGGESTION

Serve with crusty, fat-free French bread or a toasted bagel topped with jalapeño dip (page 238).

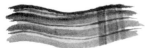

SALAD
DRESSINGS
AND SALADS

CREAMY DILL DRESSING

YIELD: 1 CUP

Bread provides a thick, creamy texture to this dressing, which may also be used as a dip for vegetable sticks. One half of a boiled, peeled, sliced potato may replace the bread (like the bread, the potato should be added gradually to the mixture). The dressing will last for one day in the refrigerator.

1 clove garlic
1 piece ginger (1 inch long), peeled and chopped, or ½ teaspoon processed ginger
4 tablespoons nonfat plain yogurt
2 tablespoons lemon juice
Salt to taste
1 cup fresh dill sprigs, rinsed and drained
1 slice white bread, torn into small pieces, plus additional as needed

Place garlic, ginger, yogurt, lemon juice, salt, and dill in a food processor and press the pulse button to puree the ingredients. Gradually add the bread pieces and process between additions until a creamy consistency is achieved. Adjust seasoning and lemon juice to taste.

Transfer dressing into a bowl, cover, and store in the refrigerator. Just before serving, mix well. Serve chilled.

EACH TABLESPOON PROVIDES
8 calories, 0.4 g protein, 1.3 g carbohydrate
0.1 g fat, 9 mg sodium, 0 mg cholesterol

SERVING SUGGESTION

Serve over a salad of chopped fresh spinach and tomato wedges.

CREAMY GARLIC DRESSING

YIELD: ½ CUP

Yogurt cheese gives this dressing a thicker and creamier consistency than plain yogurt. Yogurt cheese may be prepared a day in advance and refrigerated in a covered dish. The dressing will last four to five days in the refrigerator.

½ cup yogurt cheese (page 252)
2 tablespoons lemon juice
1 teaspoon processed onion
½ teaspoon processed garlic
Salt and pepper to taste

Mix all ingredients in a small bowl. Adjust seasoning to taste. Cover and chill.

EACH TABLESPOON PROVIDES
16 calories, 0.8 g protein, 2.2 g carbohydrate
0 g fat, 4 mg sodium, 1 mg cholesterol

SERVING SUGGESTION

Serve over a bowl of fresh tossed salad or use as a topping for baked potatoes.

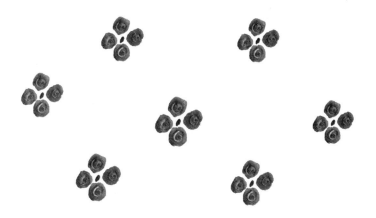

LEMON-HERB DRESSING

YIELD: ½ CUP

This classic house dressing has a water base instead
of an oil base. The arrowroot mixture thickens
the dressing to make it "stick" to the salad. This
dressing will last two weeks in an airtight jar in
the refrigerator.

4 tablespoons lemon or lime juice
2 tablespoons distilled white vinegar
⅓ cup water
¼ teaspoon processed garlic
¼ teaspoon dried basil
¼ teaspoon dried tarragon
¾ teaspoon sugar
Salt and pepper to taste
2 tablespoons water mixed with
    1 tablespoon arrowroot

In a 1-quart stainless steel or Corning glass saucepan, mix the lemon juice, vinegar, water, garlic,
basil, tarragon, sugar, salt, and pepper and simmer
on medium heat. Reduce the heat to very low and
gradually stir in the arrowroot mixture, which will

thicken the dressing. Immediately remove from heat and set aside to cool. If the cooled dressing is too thick, add 1 tablespoon water, stir, and adjust seasoning accordingly. Set aside to cool.

EACH TABLESPOON PROVIDES
8 calories, 0.1 g protein, 2.3 g carbohydrate
0 g fat, 1 mg sodium, 0 mg cholesterol

SERVING SUGGESTION

Serve over cold mushroom-spinach salad (page 58) or a tossed salad of any kind.

EGGLESS EGG SALAD

YIELD: 4 SERVINGS

Created for vegetarians, this variation of "egg salad" combines firm tofu, yogurt, and Dijon mustard for the rich, creamy taste without adding mayonnaise or egg. Tofu is rich in protein and helps lower cholesterol. The egg salad, covered and stored in the refrigerator, will last for two or three days.

$\frac{1}{2}$ pound firm lowfat tofu
$\frac{1}{2}$ cup chopped celery
$\frac{1}{4}$ cup chopped onion
$\frac{1}{2}$ cup chopped fresh cilantro or parsley,
    rinsed and drained
1 tablespoon Dijon mustard
1 tablespoon nonfat plain yogurt
Salt and black pepper to taste

In a medium-size bowl, mash the tofu with a fork (you should have about 1 cup). Add the celery, onion, cilantro, mustard, yogurt, salt, and pepper and mix well. Cover and chill.

EACH SERVING PROVIDES
40 calories, 4.8 g protein, 2.8 g carbohydrate
1.2 g fat, 175 mg sodium, 0 mg cholesterol

SERVING SUGGESTION
••
Serve on a toasted bun or toasted whole wheat bread with lettuce, tomato, and pickle.

GREEK BEAN AND ARTICHOKE SALAD

YIELD: 4 SERVINGS

Greek diners serve this salad tossed with olive oil and a generous amount of curly parsley for a robust flavor. This fat-free version of the peppy salad takes minutes to put together and is an excellent source of protein and fiber. The pickled artichokes go well with the beans.

1 (15½-ounce) can Great Northern white beans
1 (13½-ounce) can artichoke hearts
   (in water, not oil)
2 tablespoons chopped red onion,
   rinsed and drained
1 tablespoon red wine vinegar
1 tablespoon lime juice
2 tablespoons chopped curly parsley
Salt and pepper to taste

Drain and rinse the beans. Drain the artichokes and cut into 1-inch pieces. In a salad bowl, mix the beans, artichoke pieces, onion, vinegar, lime juice, parsley, salt, and pepper. Adjust seasoning to taste, cover, and chill. Serve cold or at room temperature.

EACH SERVING PROVIDES
130 calories, 8.6 g protein, 25.3 g carbohydrate
0.4 g fat, 648 mg sodium, 0 mg cholesterol

SERVING SUGGESTION

Serve with tuna kebabs (page 80), garlic toast (page 214), and cold mushroom-spinach salad (page 58).

MIXED SPROUT SALAD

YIELD: 6 SERVINGS

Mixed sprouts consisting of mung, lentil, and adzuki beans, in packed containers, are available in the produce section of most supermarkets. This nutritious salad tastes more like a crunchy relish. Serve it as an appetizer, relish, or side salad with any meal.

2 cups mixed lentil, mung, and adzuki bean
    sprouts, rinsed and drained
1 cup chopped tomatoes
¼ cup chopped onion or finely sliced scallion,
    rinsed and drained
1 cup finely diced cucumber
1 cup boiled, peeled, and finely diced potato
Salt and pepper to taste
3 tablespoons lemon juice

Mix together all ingredients in a glass bowl. Serve immediately.

EACH SERVING PROVIDES
61 calories, 3.2 g protein, 13.2 g carbohydrate
0.4 g fat, 7 mg sodium, 0 mg cholesterol

SPICY POTATO SALAD

YIELD: 2 SERVINGS

This is a spicy and much lighter variation of the regular, mayonnaise-based potato salad. Spices and seasoning should be added gradually and to taste. Paprika may replace cayenne for a milder flavor.

2 cups boiled, peeled, and diced potatoes
2 tablespoons lemon juice
½ teaspoon ground cumin
2 tablespoons finely diced red onion,
    rinsed and drained
Salt to taste
¼ teaspoon cayenne or paprika
¼ teaspoon black pepper
2 tablespoons fresh chopped cilantro

Toss all ingredients in a salad bowl. Adjust seasonings and serve.

EACH SERVING PROVIDES
148 calories, 3.3 g protein, 34.3 g carbohydrate
0.3 g fat, 10 mg sodium, 0 mg cholesterol

SERVING SUGGESTION

This dish goes well as a side salad with gourmet black-eyed peas (page 124), rice-vegetable pilaf (page 226), and mixed greens.

TANGY HAWAIIAN CABBAGE SLAW

YIELD: 6 SERVINGS

This tempting side salad is an alternative to cole slaw. Its color and crunchy flavor make it a refreshing accompaniment to a spicy meal. Since mayonnaise is not added, this salad is ideal to take along on a picnic or barbecue, as it will not spoil, but do not toss the salad and dressing together until ready to serve.

2 cups finely sliced green cabbage
1 cup grated carrot
½ cup finely diced onion, rinsed and drained
1 cup canned unsweetened pineapple chunks, drained (reserve juice)
2 tablespoons distilled white vinegar or lemon juice
Salt and black pepper to taste
Fresh parsley sprigs

Mix the cabbage, carrot, onion, and pineapple chunks in a large salad bowl. Set aside.

In a small bowl, mix vinegar, 1 tablespoon of the reserved pineapple juice, salt, and pepper.

Pour dressing over the salad and toss well. Adjust seasoning and garnish with parsley. Serve immediately.

EACH SERVING PROVIDES
36 calories, 0.7 g protein, 8.9 g carbohydrate
0.1 g fat, 11 mg sodium, 0 mg cholesterol

SERVING SUGGESTION

Serve with bean and potato patties (page 176) on a toasted bun and fruit cream (page 259) for dessert.

COLD MUSHROOM-SPINACH SALAD

YIELD: 4 SERVINGS

Fresh spinach and fresh white mushrooms are a fine contrast. Spinach may be replaced by any combination of salad greens. Grated carrots and cucumber slices may be used in place of mushrooms.

4 cups fresh chopped spinach, stems removed
1 cup sliced fresh white mushrooms
$\frac{1}{4}$ cup lemon herb dressing (page 48)

Wash and drain the spinach. In a salad bowl, arrange the spinach and top with the mushroom slices. Just before serving, add the lemon herb dressing and toss well. Serve immediately.

EACH SERVING PROVIDES
25 calories, 2.0 g protein, 5.0 g carbohydrate
0.3 g fat, 45 mg sodium, 0 mg cholesterol

SERVING SUGGESTION

Serve with Cajun-style sautéed fish (page 67), rice and green peas (page 222) and savory stuffed potatoes (page 188).

POTATO SALAD WITH CAPERS AND VINAIGRETTE

YIELD: 4 SERVINGS

For this recipe, the potatoes should not be over-cooked. Balsamic vinegar is added just before serving to retain its unique flavor. This salad is great to take to a picnic or lunch buffet.

2 tablespoons balsamic vinegar
2 tablespoons lemon juice
Salt and pepper to taste
10 small potatoes, boiled, peeled, and diced
2 tablespoons capers pickled in vinegar, drained
¼ cup finely chopped fresh parsley
¼ cup finely diced red onion, rinsed and drained

Mix the vinegar, lemon juice, salt, and pepper and set aside. In a glass bowl, mix the potatoes, capers, parsley, and onion. Just before serving, pour the vinegar dressing over the potatoes and toss well. Adjust seasoning to taste.

EACH SERVING PROVIDES
174 calories, 3.6 g protein, 39.6 g carbohydrate
0.9 g fat, 111 mg sodium, 0 mg cholesterol

TABBOULEH

YIELD: 2 SERVINGS

This timeless classic serves as both a salad and relish in Middle Eastern fare. The zesty flavor blends well with the heavily spiced meats and rustic flat breads of that region. In place of traditional olive oil, use water, lime juice, tomatoes, and cucumber to provide the moist texture to this dish.

½ cup bulghur wheat
1⅓ cups boiling water
2 tablespoons finely sliced scallion
2 tablespoons finely diced cucumber
2 tablespoons finely chopped parsley
½ cup finely chopped fresh tomatoes
¼ cup lime juice
Salt and pepper to taste

In a microwave-safe bowl, mix the bulghur and hot water and microwave on high for 5 minutes. Cover and set aside for 10 minutes. Alternatively, bring 1½ cups water to a boil in a small saucepan over high heat. Stir in bulghur and reduce heat to low. Cover and simmer for 5 minutes, stirring occasionally. Turn off heat and let sit covered for 40 minutes. Drain.

In a large bowl, combine the scallion, cucumber, parsley, tomatoes, lime juice, salt, and pepper. Add the bulghur and mix well. Adjust seasoning to taste. Serve at room temperature or chilled.

EACH SERVING PROVIDES
140 calories, 5.0 g protein, 31.9 g carbohydrate
0.7 g fat, 17 mg sodium, 0 mg cholesterol

SERVING SUGGESTION

Serve as a side salad with tuna kebabs (page 80) or potato patties stuffed with peas (page 172) and mixed greens.

FISH AND SEAFOOD

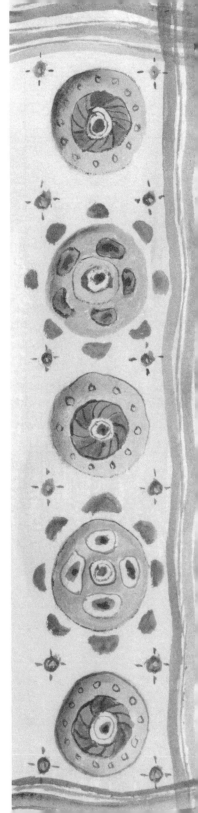

STOVE-TOP GRILLED SALMON

YIELD: 4 SERVINGS

This spicy fish is innovative and easy to make.
Cayenne may be added at the same time as
the paprika.

1 pound salmon steak
2 heaping tablespoons processed onion
1 teaspoon processed garlic
½ teaspoon cumin
½ teaspoon turmeric
½ teaspoon paprika
Salt to taste
1 tablespoon lemon juice
1 tablespoon chopped cilantro
Lemon slices

Wash the salmon and drain. Heat a nonstick pan on
medium heat, add the onion and garlic, and cook
for 4 minutes. (The onion and garlic will tend to dry
up as the juices evaporate.) Add the cumin, turmeric, paprika, salt, and lemon juice and cook for
1 minute.

Add the cilantro and salmon to the pan. Carefully spread some of the onion and spice mixture on top of the salmon. Lower heat, cover, and cook, 4 minutes. Turn the salmon over, cover pan, and cook for 3 more minutes. Turn off heat and let the fish sit in the covered pan until ready to serve.

To serve, spoon fish onto serving plate along with the spices. Garnish with lemon slices.

EACH SERVING PROVIDES

159 calories, 24.4 g protein, 3.9 g carbohydrate

4.6 g fat, 61 mg sodium, 56 mg cholesterol

SERVING SUGGESTION

Serve with savory stuffed potatoes (page 188) and quick and easy green beans (page 122).

CHUTNEY FISH

YIELD: 2 SERVINGS

Cilantro chutney is an excellent marinade for fish. The fresh black pepper and lemon juice give this dish a zesty flavor. Extra cayenne may be added to make it hotter.

½ pound fish fillet (any kind that is low in fat)
3 tablespoons tangy green cilantro chutney
   (page 232)
Fresh black pepper to taste
Dash lemon juice

Wash and drain fish. In a bowl, smear the chutney on the fish and set aside for 5 minutes. Heat a 10-inch nonstick frying pan on medium-high heat, add the fish, and pour any chutney left in the bowl over it. Sprinkle the black pepper on the fish. Lower heat to medium. Cover and cook, about 4 minutes on each side or until fish is tender, taking care fish does not burn. Add lemon juice. Serve hot.

EACH SERVING PROVIDES
103 calories, 20.5 g protein, 2.3 g carbohydrate
0.8 g fat, 72 mg sodium, 49 mg cholesterol

SERVING SUGGESTION

Serve with tofu with green and red peppers (page 200), rice and green peas (page 222), and mixed sprout salad (page 54).

Fish and Seafood

CAJUN-STYLE SAUTÉED FISH

YIELD: 4 SERVINGS

Cajun cooking—a blend of French, African, and Native American cooking techniques—was introduced in Louisiana around 1760 by the French Acadians. The French immigrants brought with them a unique culinary history and style. The African method of spicy cooking was fused with local ingredients (certain vegetables in our supermarkets today, such as yam, okra, and collard greens, were originally indigenous to Africa). The Native American culture lent the flavor of corn, herbs, and spices to this enticing cuisine.

We use tuna for this recipe, but another fish may be substituted. Keep in mind that flounder, white fish, halibut, snapper, sole, roughy, and tuna (canned in water) are lower in fat than other fish (one gram of fat per 3-ounce serving).

CONTINUED

1 pound tuna steak or any kind of fish steak
1 teaspoon paprika
¼ teaspoon ground black pepper
¼ teaspoon ground cumin
¼ teaspoon cayenne
¼ teaspoon dried thyme
¼ teaspoon dried oregano
¼ teaspoon dried basil
1 heaping tablespoon processed onion
½ teaspoon processed garlic
Juice of 1 lemon or lime
1 tablespoon distilled white vinegar
Salt to taste
Parsley
Lime wedges

Wash the fish, drain it, and set aside. In a small bowl, mix the paprika, pepper, cumin, cayenne, thyme, oregano, and basil. Place a 10-inch nonstick pan or skillet on medium heat, add the dry ingredients, stir, and roast, 30 to 50 seconds. Add the onion and garlic and stir, 1 minute. Add the fish steak, lemon juice, vinegar, and salt. Cover, reduce heat to low, and cook, about 3 minutes. Turn the steak over and cook for 5 minutes or until fish is tender. Raise heat to reduce some of the liquid. Turn onto a serving plate and spoon on the spicy juices. Serve hot topped with parsley and lime wedges.

EACH SERVING PROVIDES

203 calories, 30.9 g protein, 3.7 g carbohydrate

6.6 g fat, 52 mg sodium, 50 mg cholesterol

SERVING SUGGESTION

Serve with a green salad, baked potato topped with jalapeño dip (page 238), and garlic toast (page 214).

"GRILLED" FISH

Any lowfat fish tastes good with this spicy marinade, which can also be used for grilled fish. This
stove-top version looks and tastes the same as
grilled fish but is much quicker to prepare. The
amount of cooking time depends on the size and
thickness of the steak.

1 pound fish steak (any kind low in fat)
3 tablespoons tomato puree
1 hot green chili pepper, finely chopped
3 tablespoons lemon juice
1 teaspoon processed ginger
½ teaspoon processed garlic
2 teaspoons soy sauce
Salt to taste
Parsley
Lime wedges

Wash fish and pat dry with paper towels. In a small
bowl, mix the tomato puree, chili pepper, lemon
juice, ginger, garlic, soy sauce, and salt. Marinate the

fish in this mixture, about 20 minutes. Place a non-stick frying pan on medium-high heat, add the fish and marinade, cover, and cook on low to medium heat for 3 to 5 minutes per side. Garnish with parsley and lime wedges, and serve hot.

EACH SERVING PROVIDES
109 calories, 20.9 g protein, 4.0 g carbohydrate
0.8 g fat, 293 mg sodium, 49 mg cholesterol

SERVING SUGGESTION

Serve with elegant rice with mushrooms (page 220), gourmet potatoes and peas (page 184), and a tossed salad.

THAI FISH

YIELD: 2 SERVINGS

Almost any kind of lowfat fish may be used in this recipe. The taste is in the spicy red sauce in which the fish is simmered. For a hotter taste, a few drops of Tabasco sauce may be added. If desired, top with additional sliced green scallion for a garnish.

½ pound fish steak (any kind low in fat)
2 tablespoons finely sliced scallion
    (green ends included)
½ cup chopped red bell pepper
½ teaspoon processed garlic
1 piece fresh ginger (½ inch long), peeled and
    chopped, or ½ teaspoon processed ginger
2 tablespoons lemon juice
2 tablespoons low-sodium soy sauce
1 tablespoon hot sauce, or to taste
Nonstick cooking spray

Wash the fish and set aside to drain. Rinse the scallion in water, drain, and set aside. Process the red pepper, garlic, ginger, lemon juice, soy sauce, and hot sauce in a food processor to a pulp. Place a 10-inch nonstick frying pan on medium-high heat. When hot, spray with nonstick cooking spray, add the scallion, and cook for 1½ minutes over medium-high heat. Add the sauce and simmer for 2 more minutes. Add the fish steak and reduce heat to low. Spoon sauce over the steak, cover, and cook until fish is tender, turning it over once. Serve hot.

EACH SERVING PROVIDES
121 calories, 21.7 g protein, 5.7 g carbohydrate
1.1 g fat, 721 mg sodium, 49 mg cholesterol

SERVING SUGGESTION

Serve on plain rice, with stuffed peppers (page 182), tangy green cilantro chutney (page 232), and a tossed salad on the side.

FISH WITH TANDOORI SAUCE

YIELD: 2 SERVINGS

In India, a tandoor is a clay oven in which the temperature is very hot to seal in the juices of the piece of meat placed inside it. This recipe is prepared on the stove for convenience. A tandoori sauce is a highly spiced, tangy yogurt marinade. Even if you don't have all the spices listed below, try it with whatever you have in your spice rack.

½ pound fresh lowfat fish fillet with
   no small bones
½ teaspoon ground cumin
½ teaspoon processed garlic
½ teaspoon processed ginger
4 tablespoons nonfat plain yogurt
2 tablespoons lemon juice
¼ teaspoon ground clove
¼ teaspoon ground cinnamon
½ teaspoon paprika
Salt and freshly ground pepper to taste
1 tablespoon all-purpose flour
1 to 2 drops orange food coloring
   (you can combine red and yellow food coloring)
Nonstick cooking spray
1 tablespoon processed onion

Wash the fish, pat dry, and set aside. To create the sauce, in a bowl, mix the cumin, garlic, ginger, yogurt, lemon juice, clove, cinnamon, paprika, salt, pepper, flour, and food coloring.

Place a 10-inch or larger nonstick frying pan on high heat. When hot, spray lightly with nonstick cooking spray, add onion, and cook for 2 minutes, stirring continuously. Reduce heat, add sauce, and simmer for 2 minutes. Add the fish, baste with sauce, cover, and cook on low heat until fish is tender, turning the fish once during cooking. Raise heat to reduce sauce, if desired. Serve hot.

EACH SERVING PROVIDES
150 calories, 23.0 g protein, 10.8 g carbohydrate
1.4 g fat, 95 mg sodium, 49 mg cholesterol

SERVING SUGGESTION
••
Try potato salad with capers and vinaigrette (page 59), "creamed" spinach (page 138), and white rice with this preparation.

TOMATO FISH WITH BLACK MUSTARD SEEDS

YIELD: 2 SERVINGS

Heat induces the mustard seeds to pop and emit a spicy flavor, which, when combined with the thyme, vinegar, and fresh cilantro, is a perfect seasoning for this recipe. Fish steaks require a few minutes longer to cook than fish fillets. To make preparation easier, have all ingredients measured and on hand before you start cooking.

½ pound fresh lowfat fish fillet or steak with
    no small bones
½ teaspoon black mustard seeds
½ teaspoon dried thyme
1 teaspoon processed garlic
2 small hot green chilies, or to taste,
    finely chopped
¼ cup distilled white vinegar
½ cup tomato puree
¼ cup fresh cilantro, finely chopped
Salt to taste
Cilantro sprigs

Wash the fish, pat dry, and set aside. Heat a 10-inch nonstick frying pan on medium-high heat. Add the mustard seeds. When seeds begin to pop, add the thyme, garlic, chilies, vinegar, and tomato puree. Cook for 1 minute, then add the fish, cilantro, and salt. Spoon sauce over the fish. Lower heat, cover, and cook until fish is tender, gently turning once and spooning sauce over the fish. Top with sprigs of cilantro. Serve hot.

EACH SERVING PROVIDES
149 calories, 22.5 g protein, 13.9 g carbohydrate
1.1 g fat, 330 mg sodium, 49 mg cholesterol

SERVING SUGGESTION

Serve with spinach-potato toss-up (page 198), savory yellow rice (page 228), and Greek bean and artichoke salad (page 54) for a complete meal.

FILLET OF FISH WITH SPICY STUFFING

YIELD: 4 SERVINGS

Spicy, processed chickpeas are stuffed inside a fillet of fish and cooked in this variation of stuffed flounder. Taste and adjust spices and seasoning in the chickpea mixture before stuffing.

1 pound fillet of fish (any kind)
1 cup canned chickpeas, rinsed and drained
2 hot green chili peppers, or 1 jalapeño pepper, sliced with stem and seeds removed
3 tablespoons fresh cilantro leaves
½ teaspoon processed garlic
1 teaspoon processed or freshly grated ginger
3 tablespoons lemon juice or to taste
Salt to taste
Nonstick cooking spray
Paprika
Parsley
Lemon or lime wedges

Wash the fish fillet, pat dry, and set aside. Process the chickpeas, chili peppers, cilantro, garlic, ginger, lemon juice, and salt to a paste in the food processor. Set a nonstick pan on medium heat. When hot, spray with nonstick cooking spray and add the chickpea mixture. Cook on medium heat for about 4 minutes, stirring continuously to prevent sticking and lowering heat if necessary. Remove from heat and set aside.

Lay the fish flat on a cutting board. Spoon 2 tablespoons of the chickpea mixture on one end of the fillet, and starting with that end, roll the fish up like a jelly roll. Secure with a toothpick pierced through the center. Place the fish rolls on a microwave-safe dish lined with paper towels. Sprinkle with the paprika. Cover with a paper towel and microwave on high for 5 minutes. Or preheat oven to 450 degrees F, wrap rolled fish in foil, place on a baking dish, and bake for 35 minutes.

Carefully place the cooked fish rolls onto a serving dish and garnish with parsley and lemon wedges. Serve hot.

EACH SERVING PROVIDES
180 calories, 23.7 g protein, 17.2 g carbohydrate
1.7 g fat, 195 mg sodium, 49 mg cholesterol

SERVING SUGGESTION
Serve on a bed of wilted Korean spinach (page 208) with appetizing mushroom and peas (page 162), white rice, and a baked potato.

TUNA KEBABS

YIELD: 18 COCKTAIL-SIZE KEBABS

Canned tuna is used to make these spicy kebabs, which can be served with green chutney or jalapeño dip. Make the kebabs burger-size for a great sandwich filling or to stuff into pita bread with shredded lettuce and chopped tomato. They can be made ahead of time, stored in the refrigerator for up to two days, and reheated in the microwave before serving.

2 (6½-ounce) cans chunk light tuna in water
1 cup chopped onion, rinsed and drained
2 egg whites
1 slice white bread plus additional as needed
3 cloves garlic, peeled
½ teaspoon ground cumin
¼ teaspoon ground cloves
¼ teaspoon ground cinnamon
1 hot green chili pepper
2 tablespoons lemon juice or to taste
3 tablespoons chopped cilantro leaves
Salt and pepper to taste
1 cup whole wheat flour
Nonstick cooking spray

Drain the tuna thoroughly in a strainer, pressing out as much water as possible with the back of a spoon.

In a food processor, blend the tuna, onion, egg whites, bread, garlic, cumin, cloves, cinnamon, chili pepper, lemon juice, cilantro, salt, and pepper. If the mixture is too moist, crumble another slice of bread, add to the mixture, and process again (the bread will absorb the excess moisture and help in binding). Adjust salt and lemon juice to taste. Shape the mixture into 16 to 18 equal-size patties, 1½ inches in diameter. Coat patties in flour, cover with a paper towel, and set aside.

Heat a large non-stick frying pan on medium-high heat. When hot, spray evenly with nonstick cooking spray and add as many patties as will fit without crowding. Cook until golden brown on both sides. Place on a warmed platter and serve hot.

EACH SERVING PROVIDES
58 calories, 6.3 g protein, 7.4 g carbohydrate
0.4 g fat, 74 mg sodium, 5 mg cholesterol

SERVING SUGGESTION
....
Serve as an appetizer, with jalapeño dip (page 238) or tangy green cilantro chutney (page 232), or as a sandwich filler in a bun with hot sauce or ketchup.

CRAB CAKES WITH SCALLION AND HERBS

YIELD: 8 CRAB CAKES

An excellent sandwich filler, these cakes can be stored a couple of days in the refrigerator and heated before serving. To be able to shape crab meat into cakes, discard as much liquid as possible from the crab meat. The egg white, bread, and mashed potatoes work as "binders." Handle the crab cakes gently when browning, as they tend to break; they will become firm after cooking.

1 (6-ounce) can crab meat, drained
1 finely sliced scallion
2 tablespoons finely diced celery
1 egg white
2 tablespoons lemon juice
2 tablespoons chopped cilantro
1 slice white bread
Salt and pepper to taste
1 medium potato plus additional if necessary,
    boiled, peeled, and mashed
¼ cup whole wheat flour
Nonstick cooking spray

Squeeze out as much water as possible from the crab meat. In a bowl, mix the crab meat, scallion, celery, egg white, lemon juice, and cilantro. Crumble the bread and add to the mixture. Add salt and pepper. Add as much mashed potato as needed to bind the mixture. Form into small cakes, 2 inches in diameter. Lightly dust the cakes with whole wheat flour and set aside on a plate.

Place a 12-inch nonstick frying pan on medium-high heat. When hot, spray evenly with nonstick cooking spray and add as many crab cakes as will fit without crowding the pan. Lightly brown the crab cakes on both sides, turning over carefully, using two implements to avoid breakage. Serve hot.

EACH SERVING PROVIDES

62 calories, 6.1 g protein, 8.5 g carbohydrate

0.5 g fat, 95 mg sodium, 19 mg cholesterol

SERVING SUGGESTION

Serve as an appetizer with tangy green cilantro chutney (page 232) or in a toasted bun with hot sauce.

POULTRY
AND EGGS

SPANISH-STYLE CHICKEN WITH PEPPERS

YIELD: 8 SERVINGS

The traditional cooking of Spain and Portugal makes liberal use of lard, smoked ham, and black and green olives to lend flavor to this festive dish. Our light version creates this spectacular entrée with a combination of red and green peppers, a dash of hot sauce, garlic, and onions and tops it with a few black olives (olives contain some fat, so their use as a garnish is limited).

6 heaping tablespoons processed onion
1½ teaspoons processed garlic
4 tablespoons tomato puree
Salt to taste
1 heaping teaspoon paprika
1½ pounds boneless, skinless chicken thighs
    (visible fat trimmed), cut into 10 pieces
    (2½ inches each)
½ cup sliced red bell pepper (2-inch slices)
½ cup sliced green bell pepper (2-inch slices)
2 tablespoons hot sauce, or to taste
3 large pitted black olives, drained and sliced

In a large stainless steel pot, mix the onion, garlic, tomato puree, salt, and paprika to make a marinade. Add the chicken pieces and mix well. Cover and cook on low heat, about 35 minutes or until chicken is just tender. Add the red and green peppers and hot sauce. Raise heat to medium-high and stir briskly, about 5 minutes or until the peppers are crisp-tender and the sauce is reduced. Remove the chicken and peppers to a serving dish, spoon on the sauce, and top with sliced olives. Serve hot.

EACH SERVING PROVIDES
130 calories, 17.6 g protein, 6.1 g carbohydrate
3.7 g fat, 139 mg sodium, 70 mg cholesterol

SERVING SUGGESTION

Serve with white rice and a mixed green salad.

CHICKEN CACCIATORE

YIELD: 8 SERVINGS

Italian cuisine rates as one of the world's most popular, and this lowfat version of a classic is one of the reasons.

2 pounds boneless, skinless chicken thighs
    (visible fat trimmed), cut into 2-inch pieces
6 heaping tablespoons processed onion
2 teaspoons processed garlic
6 tablespoons tomato puree
1 teaspoon paprika
4 tablespoons red wine vinegar
½ teaspoon dried oregano
½ teaspoon dried basil
½ teaspoon dried thyme
Salt and pepper to taste
Fresh basil

Mix the chicken, onion, garlic, tomato puree, paprika, vinegar, dried oregano, dried basil, dried thyme, salt, and pepper in a 6-quart stainless steel pot. Cover and bring to a boil on high heat. Reduce heat to low and cook for 30 minutes or until chicken is tender. Serve hot, garnished with fresh basil.

EACH SERVING PROVIDES
162 calories, 23.2 g protein, 6.4 g carbohydrate
4.6 g fat, 145 mg sodium, 93 mg cholesterol

SERVING SUGGESTION

Serve on a bed of linguine along with a green salad and slices of garlic toast (page 214).

THAI CHICKEN

YIELD: 4 SERVINGS

Thailand, like other countries of the Far East, was known for economical one-pot cooking, which combined meat and vegetables, to stretch the dish. One-step cooking works well with a healthy lifestyle and also saves time. Thai food can be made mild or hot to taste.

½ pound skinless chicken legs or thighs
   (visible fat trimmed), cut into 6 pieces
   (3 inches each)
1 fresh hot serrano or jalapeño chili pepper
1 medium onion, peeled and chopped
½ teaspoon cayenne, or to taste
1 teaspoon ground coriander
1 (1-inch) piece of ginger, peeled and sliced
1½ teaspoons processed garlic
4 tablespoons lemon or lime juice
1 cup fresh cilantro leaves
½ cup sliced fresh snow peas
½ cup sliced canned water chestnuts (drained)
½ cup sliced fresh mushrooms
Salt to taste

Wash and drain the chicken, and set aside.

Combine the chili pepper, onion, cayenne, coriander, ginger, garlic, lemon juice, and cilantro and process in a food processor to form a paste.

In a 6-quart stainless steel pot, combine the chicken and paste. Set the pot on low heat, cover, and cook for 35 minutes or until chicken is tender. Add the snow peas, water chestnuts, mushrooms, and salt. Raise heat and stir briskly for 5 minutes or until vegetables are crisp-tender and liquid is slightly reduced. Remove to a serving dish. Serve hot.

EACH SERVING PROVIDES

101 calories, 10.2 g protein, 11.3 g carbohydrate

2.0 g fat, 49 mg sodium, 34 mg cholesterol

SERVING SUGGESTION

Serve with white rice, stuffed peppers (page 182), and cold mushroom-spinach salad (page 58).

CHICKEN WITH TANDOORI SAUCE

YIELD: 8 SERVINGS

The rich, subtle, and satisfying flavor of this dish will be remembered long after the meal is over. This is a dish for any occasion. For those who are lactose-intolerant, the yogurt may be replaced with tomato puree.

2 pounds boneless, skinless chicken thighs (visible fat trimmed), cut into 2-inch pieces
½ cup nonfat plain yogurt
8 heaping tablespoons processed onion
1½ teaspoons processed garlic
1 teaspoon paprika
¼ teaspoon ground clove
¼ teaspoon ground cinnamon
1 teaspoon ground cumin
Salt and pepper to taste
2 tablespoons lemon juice
1 rounded tablespoon all-purpose flour
Sliced fresh green chili peppers

Wash and drain the chicken. In a 6-quart stainless steel pot, combine the chicken, yogurt, onion, garlic, paprika, clove, cinnamon, cumin, salt, pepper, lemon juice, and flour. Mix well. Cover and cook on low heat for 35 to 40 minutes or until chicken is tender. If sauce needs to be reduced, remove cover, raise heat, and cook briskly for 2 to 3 minutes. Remove chicken to a serving dish with the tandoori sauce over it and top with slices of chili peppers.

EACH SERVING PROVIDES
175 calories, 24.0 g protein, 8.1 g carbohydrate
4.7 g fat, 108 mg sodium, 94 mg cholesterol

SERVING SUGGESTION

Serve with warm pita bread or white rice, spicy mixed vegetables (page 196), and tangy Hawaiian cabbage slaw (page 56), or serve with warm whole wheat pita bread, homemade pickled onions (page 242), and savory chickpeas (page 134).

POT LUCKY CHICKEN

YIELD: 8 SERVINGS

Boneless and skinless chicken thighs work very well in this effortless preparation.

2 pounds boneless, skinless chicken thighs
   (visible fat trimmed), cut into 1½-inch pieces
8 heaping tablespoons processed onion
2 heaping teaspoons processed garlic
1½ teaspoons processed ginger
2 tablespoons distilled white vinegar
Salt to taste
½ teaspoon turmeric
½ teaspoon ground cinnamon
¼ teaspoon ground clove
¼ teaspoon ground cardamom
½ teaspoon paprika
3 small potatoes, boiled, peeled, and halved
½ cup cooked green peas

Wash chicken and drain. Combine the chicken, onion, garlic, ginger, vinegar, salt, turmeric, cinnamon, clove, cardamom, and paprika in a 6-quart stainless steel pot. Cover and cook on low heat for 40 minutes, stirring chicken once or twice, until the chicken is tender. Remove chicken with a slotted spoon to a serving dish and cover. Add the potatoes to the pot and gently toss for 2 minutes until they are coated with the chicken gravy and are heated through. Spoon the potatoes and gravy on top of the chicken. Arrange peas around the chicken. Serve hot.

EACH SERVING PROVIDES

195 calories, 24.1 g protein, 13.2 g carbohydrate

4.7 g fat, 107 mg sodium, 93 mg cholesterol

SERVING SUGGESTION

Serve with rice, pickled onions (page 242), and a tossed salad.

CLASSIC CHICKEN CURRY

YIELD: 8 SERVINGS

This splendid all-time favorite from the heartland of northern India, prepared with fat-free ingredients, loses none of its flavor. It can be made mild or hot to taste. (Incidentally, authentic curry is never made with curry powder. The trick is in dry-roasting spices to just the right degree.) This dish keeps well in the freezer or refrigerator. The spices, over time, permeate into the meat and add to the flavor. If refrigerated overnight, any visible fat on the surface can be skimmed to make it leaner. For those who are lactose-intolerant, omit the yogurt.

2 pounds boneless, skinless chicken thighs (visible fat trimmed), cut into 1½-inch pieces
1 teaspoon ground cumin
1 teaspoon ground coriander
1 teaspoon turmeric
8 heaping tablespoons processed onion
2 teaspoons processed ginger
1 teaspoon processed garlic
3 tablespoons nonfat plain yogurt
4 tablespoons crushed tomatoes or tomato puree or tomato juice
¼ teaspoon ground clove
¼ teaspoon ground cardamom
¼ teaspoon cayenne, or to taste
1 tablespoon paprika

½ cup water
Salt to taste
Cilantro or parsley

Wash chicken, pat dry, and set aside. Place a 6-quart stainless steel pot over medium heat. Add the cumin, coriander, and turmeric and stir for 2 minutes. Reduce heat to low and immediately add the onion, ginger, and garlic. Increase heat to medium and stir for 3 to 4 minutes (the mixture will start sticking to the pot). Gradually add the yogurt and tomatoes, constantly stirring. Add the clove, cardamom, cayenne, paprika, and chicken. Wash chicken, pat dry, and add to the pot. Stir for about 4 minutes to ensure that all ingredients are well mixed. Add the water and salt and stir well. Cover and cook on low heat, about 30 minutes or until chicken is tender and the curry turns a reddish brown. Transfer to a serving bowl and garnish with chopped cilantro or parsley sprigs.

EACH SERVING PROVIDES
172 calories, 23.7 g protein, 7.7 g carbohydrate
4.8 g fat, 131 mg sodium, 94 mg cholesterol

SERVING SUGGESTION

White rice, spicy eggplant (page 144), green salad, and homemade pickled onions (page 242) make this an interesting and balanced feast.

CHICKEN KEBABS YUM YUM

YIELD: 10 KEBABS

Kebabs are usually made with cubes of meat or ground meat. This recipe is a good way to recycle leftover roasted or grilled chicken.

2 cups boneless, skinless, cooked chicken cut
    into 1-inch pieces
½ cup chopped onions, rinsed and drained
2 cloves garlic
1 teaspoon processed ginger
Salt and pepper to taste
¼ teaspoon ground clove
¼ teaspoon ground cinnamon
2 tablespoons chopped cilantro
1 egg white
1 tablespoon lemon juice or to taste
1 cup whole wheat flour
Nonstick cooking spray

Process the chicken, onions, garlic, ginger, salt, pepper, clove, cinnamon, cilantro, egg white, and lemon juice to a paste in a food processor. Shape into patties, each about 2 inches in diameter and ¼ inch thick, and coat with whole wheat flour. Heat a nonstick frying pan over medium-high heat. When hot, spray lightly with nonstick cooking spray and add as many patties as will fit comfortably. Brown on both sides and transfer finished patties to a warmed platter while cooking the remainder. Serve hot.

EACH SERVING PROVIDES
101 calories, 10.2 g protein, 10.0 g carbohydrate
2.4 g fat, 31 mg sodium, 25 mg cholesterol

SERVING SUGGESTION

Serve topped with tangy green cilantro chutney (page 232) or hot sauce for appetizers, or serve on whole wheat toasted buns with lettuce and tomato for an appetizing lunch.

CHICKEN BIRYANI

YIELD: 10 SERVINGS

Biryani, a legacy of the Persian style of cooking in the 1500s, is a dish in which the spicy meat and saffron rice are arranged in layers and steamed so that their flavors fuse. The original recipe, which is very rich in fat, was prepared on festive occasions for kings and their royal guests. This lowfat version, with a garnish of dried fruit, looks and tastes every bit as authentic.

The chicken and rice may be prepared a day or two ahead of time and refrigerated. Before assembling, the chicken must be simmered on the stove to ensure it is well heated before it is layered with the rice. If the chicken gravy has thickened in the refrigerator, add a quarter cup of water and heat through. Adjust the salt accordingly.

The Rice
1½ cups basmati rice
2¼ cups water
2 cinnamon sticks
2 whole cloves
3 cardamom pods
2 bay leaves

The Chicken
2 pounds boneless, skinless chicken thighs
   (visible fat trimmed), cut into 1½-inch cubes
3 heaping tablespoons processed onion

1 tablespoon processed garlic
1 teaspoon processed ginger
¼ teaspoon ground clove
¼ teaspoon ground cinnamon
¼ teaspoon ground cardamom
¼ teaspoon ground nutmeg
Salt and pepper to taste
3 tablespoons tomato puree
2 tablespoons nonfat plain yogurt

The Assembly
2 tablespoons skim milk
8 threads saffron
Orange food coloring (you can combine red and
    yellow food coloring)
Salt to taste
¾ cup nonfat plain yogurt
1 tablespoon golden raisins
1 tablespoon chopped apricots
1 tablespoon chopped, pitted dates
2 eggs, hard-boiled (yolk removed), shelled,
    and sliced
2 tablespoons chopped cilantro

Gently rinse and drain the rice. Put the rice, water,
cinnamon, cloves, cardamom, and bay leaves in a
saucepan on high heat and bring to a boil. Cover,
turn heat to low, and cook for about 15 minutes or
until all water is absorbed. Turn off the heat, discard
whole spices, and set aside, still covered.

CONTINUED

Wash and drain chicken pieces. In a 6-quart stainless steel pot, mix the chicken, onion, garlic, ginger, clove, cinnamon, cardamom, nutmeg, salt, pepper, tomato puree, and yogurt. Cover and cook on low heat for 30 minutes or until the chicken is tender and about 1 cup of the gravy is left. If too much liquid remains, raise the heat to high to reduce the liquid and stir constantly to ensure that the chicken does not burn or stick. Cover and set aside (or refrigerate after cooling for later use).

To prepare the biryani, combine the milk and saffron in a small bowl, microwave for 30 seconds, and set aside. Alternatively, warm milk and saffron in small saucepan over low heat. If the chicken has been prepared ahead of time and refrigerated, simmer it on the stove on low heat until warm. Mix the orange food coloring and salt with the yogurt. Divide the rice in half. In a bowl, mix half of the rice with the colored yogurt so that the rice is a bright orange color.

In a deep, microwave-safe pie dish, arrange one layer of orange rice, then a layer of chicken, spooning some of the gravy on it. Add one layer of white rice and one layer of chicken, and so on, until all the rice and chicken have been placed alternately in layers. (The number of layers do not matter, nor does it matter whether the top layer is rice or chicken.) Sprinkle the milk mixed with saffron over the top and inside edge of the layered dish. If cooking the biryani in the microwave, cover dish snugly with a lid or plastic wrap and microwave the biryani on high for 4 minutes. If cooking in the oven, preheat oven to 350 degrees F. Cover the biryani with foil and bake for about 20 minutes. The generated steam will combine the flavors of the chicken and rice.

Mix the raisins, apricots, dates, and 2 tablespoons water in a small bowl and microwave for 1 minute to steam the fruit or put dried fruit and water in a small saucepan and simmer over low heat for 2 minutes. Drain the water. Invert and unmold the biryani dish onto a fancy serving platter and garnish with the steamed fruit, sliced egg whites, and chopped cilantro.

EACH SERVING PROVIDES
250 calories, 22.4 g protein, 29.8 g carbohydrate
3.9 g fat, 129 mg sodium, 76 mg cholesterol

SERVING SUGGESTION
••
A simple cold cucumber yogurt relish (page 248), green salad, and lime pickle (page 244) are ideal accompaniments to this festive preparation.

GROUND TURKEY WITH PEAS

YIELD: 6 SERVINGS

A combination of spices are used to add flavor to ground turkey, which replaces ground beef in this recipe.

1 teaspoon ground cumin
1 teaspoon turmeric
2 teaspoons processed garlic
4 heaping tablespoons processed onion
5 tablespoons tomato puree
½ teaspoon ground cinnamon
½ teaspoon ground nutmeg
½ teaspoon chili powder
1 pound ground turkey
¼ cup distilled white vinegar
½ cup water
1 cup frozen peas

Place a 6-quart stainless saucepan on medium-high heat. Add cumin and turmeric and stir for 1 minute or until the pan begins to smoke very slightly around the sides. Immediately add the garlic and onion, lower heat to medium, and stir for about 4 minutes. If the mixture begins to stick during the cooking time, reduce heat and add the tomato puree, one tablespoon at a time, continually stirring. Alternatively, add the tomato puree after the garlic-onion mixture is cooked. Add the cinnamon, nutmeg, chili powder, and ground turkey. Add the vinegar and water and mix well. Cover and simmer on low heat, about 15 minutes or until the turkey is cooked. Add the peas and cook for another 3 minutes. Serve hot.

EACH SERVING PROVIDES
159 calories, 15.6 g protein, 10.6 g carbohydrate
6.1 g fat, 148 mg sodium, 56 mg cholesterol

SERVING SUGGESTION

Serve over a bed of white rice, with spicy mixed vegetables (page 196) and homemade pickled onions (page 242) on the side.

DEVILED EGGS WITH TUNA FILLING

YIELD: 6 SERVINGS

A traditional buffet generally has some form of stuffed hard-boiled eggs. This version eliminates the egg yolks and adds tuna.

6 large eggs, hard-boiled and shelled
1 (6½-ounce) can chunk white tuna
   (packed in water)
1 teaspoon prepared Dijon mustard
2 cloves garlic
3 tablespoons lime juice
Salt and pepper to taste
¼ cup fresh parsley

Slice the eggs in half lengthwise and carefully discard the yolk. Set egg white hollows aside. Drain the canned tuna, removing excess water by pressing it with the back of a spoon against the colander.

Process the tuna, mustard, garlic, lime juice, salt, and pepper in a food processor to a puree. Adjust seasoning. Spoon or pipe the tuna mixture into the hollowed eggs. Garnish with parsley and serve at room temperature or chilled.

EACH SERVING PROVIDES
62 calories, 11.5 g protein, 1.6 g carbohydrate
0.9 g fat, 195 mg sodium, 12 mg cholesterol

SERVING SUGGESTION

Serve as an appetizer, or make a whole meal with asparagus-mushroom crostini (page 212) and mixed greens.

DEVILED EGGS WITH HERB FILLING

YIELD: 6 SERVINGS

This vegetarian filling gets its flavor from the fresh herbs. The strong flavor of parsley and dill fuse well together.

6 large eggs, hard-boiled and shelled
1 large baking potato, boiled, peeled, and chopped
1 tablespoon nonfat plain yogurt
1 tablespoon curly parsley
5 sprigs fresh dill, or ½ teaspoon dried dill
1 clove garlic
2 tablespoons lemon juice
Salt and pepper to taste
Fresh herbs such as additional parsley and dill

Slice the eggs in half lengthwise and carefully discard the yolk. Set egg white hollows aside. Process the potato, yogurt, parsley, dill, garlic, lemon juice, salt, and pepper to a puree in a food processor.

Adjust seasoning and herbs to taste. Pipe or spoon the potato-herb mixture into the hollowed eggs and garnish with sprigs of fresh herbs. Serve at room temperature.

EACH SERVING PROVIDES
60 calories, 4.6 g protein, 10.2 g carbohydrate
0.1 g fat, 59 mg sodium, 0 mg cholesterol

SERVING SUGGESTION

Take along for a picnic lunch or serve as a side dish with "grilled" fish (page 70) and appetizing mushrooms and peas (page 162).

DEVILED EGGS WITH TOFU-HERB FILLING

YIELD: 6 SERVINGS

Egg yolk is replaced with a tofu-based herb filling. The herbs are interchangeable, and fresh dill can replace cilantro and parsley. This is ideal buffet or picnic fare.

6 large eggs, hard-boiled and shelled
1 piece extra-firm lowfat tofu, 3 inches by 2 inches by ½ inch, drained
1 tablespoon nonfat plain yogurt
1 clove garlic
4 leaves fresh basil
¼ cup fresh parsley
¼ cup fresh cilantro leaves
Juice of ½ lemon
Salt and pepper to taste
Fresh herbs or paprika

Slice the eggs in half lengthwise and carefully discard the yolk. Set egg white hollows aside. Process the tofu, yogurt, garlic, basil, parsley, cilantro, lemon juice, salt, and pepper to a puree in a food processor. If the puree is too watery to handle, add more tofu and process (or, if handy, add a small boiled, peeled potato and process). Adjust seasoning. Spoon into egg hollows. Garnish with sprigs of herb or sprinkled paprika. Serve chilled or at room temperature.

EACH SERVING PROVIDES
27 calories, 4.7 g protein, 1.5 g carbohydrate
0.2 g fat, 72 mg sodium, 0 mg cholesterol

SERVING SUGGESTION

Serve with asparagus-mushroom crostini (page 212) and mixed greens to make a wholesome meal.

HERB OMELET

YIELD: 1 SERVING

Cilantro, green pepper, and scallion mixed with the egg whites give a deliciously different flavor to this omelet. Chopped mushrooms may also be added.

4 egg whites
2 tablespoons chopped fresh cilantro leaves
1 tablespoon finely sliced scallion
1 tablespoon finely diced green bell pepper
1 small hot chili pepper, seeded (optional)
Salt and pepper to taste
Nonstick cooking spray

Place egg whites, cilantro, scallion, bell pepper, chili pepper, salt and pepper in a bowl and beat lightly. Heat a 10-inch nonstick frying pan on medium heat. When hot, spray lightly with nonstick cooking spray and pour in egg mixture. Cook until the eggs set. Fold one half over the other with a spatula and turn over to cook the other side. Serve hot.

EACH SERVING PROVIDES
75 calories, 14.3 g protein, 2.3 g carbohydrate
0.2 g fat, 226 mg sodium, 0 mg cholesterol

SERVING SUGGESTION
Top with hot sauce and serve with hash browns (page 150), whole wheat toast, and fruit salad.

PORTUGUESE-STYLE EGGS WITH VEGETABLES

YIELD: 4 SERVINGS

The Portuguese make exotic use of eggs combined with vegetables and fresh cilantro in their cuisine. It is not uncommon to top sausages and spicy vegetables with eggs and bake them for an appetizing main course. In this case, egg whites are cooked in the microwave and added to the platter to reduce cooking time. Eggs may be omitted to make this a vegetarian recipe. You may need more or less vegetables, depending on the size of the platter.

$\frac{1}{2}$ teaspoon cumin seeds
1 heaping tablespoon processed onion
2 cups frozen peas
Salt to taste
2 tablespoons chopped fresh cilantro
10 small boiled potatoes, peeled and cut into
$\frac{1}{8}$-inch-thick slices
2 medium tomatoes, sliced
Nonstick cooking spray
2 egg whites
Salt and pepper to taste
Lemon juice to taste
Ketchup or Tabasco sauce

CONTINUED

Place a 3-quart stainless steel saucepan on medium heat and add cumin seeds. Roast for 1 minute or until the seeds begin to pop and crackle. Stir in the onion and cook, 2 minutes. Stir in the peas and add salt to taste. Cover, reduce heat to low, and cook for 2 minutes. Mix in 1 tablespoon of the cilantro. Remove from heat and set aside.

In a circular microwave-safe plate or platter, arrange the potato slices with occasional tomato slices in a ring, on the outer rim of the plate, each slice slightly overlapping the other. Arrange a ring of peas inside the potato-tomato ring. Fill up the center of the plate with potatoes. Cover and microwave on high, about 1 minute, to heat through, or heat in a warmed oven. Set aside.

Spray a microwave-safe flat dish or plate with non-stick cooking spray and gently place the egg whites in it. Cover and microwave until the eggs are just set and turn opaque. Alternatively, place a 6- or 8-inch nonstick pan over medium-high heat. When hot, spray with nonstick cooking spray and add egg whites, tipping the pan to spread the whites. Cook until firm. With a spatula, gently transfer the eggs onto the center of the plate, over the warmed potato slices. Season the potatoes and eggs with salt, pepper, and lemon juice. Garnish with the remaining 1 tablespoon of cilantro. Serve hot, with a dash of ketchup or Tabasco sauce.

EACH SERVING PROVIDES
238 calories, 9.7 g protein, 49.1 g carbohydrate
0.9 g fat, 112 mg sodium, 0 mg cholesterol

SERVING SUGGESTION

Serve with whole wheat toast and cold mushroom-spinach salad (page 58).

VEGETARIAN
DISHES

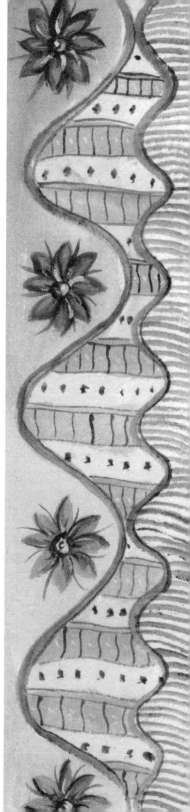

YUMMY BAKED BEANS

YIELD: 2 SERVINGS

The style of cooking baked beans varies from one family to another across America. In this version, canned pink, pinto, or red beans will all work well. Dill or parsley may be used in place of the cilantro, but salt should be added sparingly due to the high salt content in the soy sauce and hot sauce.

Nonstick cooking spray
½ cup chopped onion, rinsed and drained
¼ teaspoon garlic powder
1 fresh hot green chili pepper, finely chopped
½ cup tomato puree
1 cup finely diced green bell pepper
1 (15-ounce) can pink, pinto, or red beans,
    drained and rinsed
Salt to taste
1 tablespoon low-sodium soy sauce, or to taste
Dash Tabasco sauce or hot sauce
1 tablespoon chopped cilantro

Place a 3-quart stainless steel saucepan on medium heat for 1 minute. Spray evenly with nonstick cooking spray, add the onion and garlic powder, and stir for 2 minutes. Mix in the chili pepper, tomato puree, green pepper, beans, and salt. Lower heat, cover, and simmer for 4 minutes. The peppers should be crisp-tender. Add the soy sauce, Tabasco sauce, and cilantro. Serve hot.

EACH SERVING PROVIDES
228 calories, 12.9 g protein, 44.7 g carbohydrate
1.1 g fat, 787 mg sodium, 0 mg cholesterol

SERVING SUGGESTION

Serve on fat-free whole wheat toast or over rice with a green salad.

MEXICAN-STYLE BEAN BURRITOS

YIELD: 2 SERVINGS

Fat-free tortillas are now being introduced in supermarkets across the country, but if they are not available, you can use regular flour or whole wheat tortillas. Canned fat-free refried beans are an option; however, the amount of added sugar and artificial flavor does not make for very healthy eating. Fat-free cheddar cheese may be used sparingly.

1 (15-ounce) can pinto beans, rinsed and drained
½ teaspoon ground cumin
2 tablespoons processed onion
6 tablespoons tomato puree
Salt to taste
2 tablespoons finely chopped cilantro leaves
4 fat-free flour tortillas (9 inches in diameter)
2 tablespoons fat-free cheddar cheese (optional)

Process the beans in a food processor to form a coarse puree, adding a little water to help process the mixture. Heat a 3-quart stainless steel saucepan on medium-high heat. Add the cumin and stir for 40 seconds. Add the onion and cook for 1 minute. Reduce heat and stir in the bean puree, tomato puree, and salt. Cover and cook for 5 minutes. Remove from heat, mix in the cilantro, and set aside.

Warm the tortillas according to package directions. Place 2 tablespoons of the bean mixture in the center of each tortilla and sprinkle on a ½ tablespoon of grated cheese. Roll, tucking in ends. To microwave, place seam-side down on a microwave-safe dish, cover, and microwave on high for 40 seconds or until the burrito is heated through. To heat in the oven, preheat oven to 400 degrees F, wrap burritos individually in foil, and bake for 20 minutes. Serve hot.

EACH SERVING PROVIDES
368 calories, 15.9 g protein, 81.2 g carbohydrate
1.7 g fat, 956 mg sodium, 0 mg cholesterol

SERVING SUGGESTION

Serve burritos topped with jalapeño dip (page 238), mock guacamole (page 236), shredded lettuce, chopped tomatoes, and grated carrots.

QUICK AND EASY GREEN BEANS

YIELD: 2 SERVINGS

Flavorful, wholesome, and quick! For an easy dish, this is a recipe to remember, especially as a hearty accompaniment to any meat or pasta entrée. Fresh or frozen beans may be used (no water is required to microwave frozen beans, while fresh beans may need ½ tablespoon of water).

2 cups frozen cut green beans or fresh green beans
    cut in halves
Nonstick cooking spray
1 teaspoon processed garlic
1 tablespoon lemon juice
Salt and pepper to taste

To prepare beans in the microwave, place in a microwave-safe dish and cook on high for about 4 minutes or until crisp-tender; drain (if necessary), and set aside. Place a 4-quart stainless steel saucepan over medium heat. When hot, spray lightly with nonstick cooking spray and add the garlic;

stir to a light brown color. Add the microwaved beans, lemon juice, salt, and pepper and stir for 1 minute. If beans have not been microwaved, add frozen or fresh beans with lemon juice, salt, and pepper and cook for 7 minutes or until crisp-tender. Serve warm.

EACH SERVING PROVIDES
46 calories, 2.2 g protein, 10.4 g carbohydrate
0.5 g fat, 13 mg sodium, 0 mg cholesterol

SERVING SUGGESTION

Serve with penne pasta with basil-mushroom sauce (page 168) and garlic toast (page 214).

GOURMET BLACK-EYED PEAS

YIELD: 2 SERVINGS

A very rich source of protein and fiber, black-eyed peas are actually beans of a certain kind. This dish can be prepared in minutes and is delicious served over rice. Spices, along with processed garlic and onion, bring out the flavor of the beans; cayenne may be added to make it hot. Have all ingredients measured and on hand, since this is very quick cooking.

1 teaspoon ground cumin
1 teaspoon turmeric
2 heaping tablespoons processed onion
1 teaspoon processed garlic
4 tablespoons tomato puree
1 (15-ounce) can black-eyed peas,
    rinsed and drained
2 tablespoons lime juice or to taste
Salt to taste
2 tablespoons chopped fresh cilantro leaves

Place a 3-quart stainless steel saucepan on medium-high heat. Add the cumin and turmeric and stir, 1 minute or until it just begins to smoke (the turmeric will turn orange-brown); do not allow it to burn. Immediately reduce the heat to low and add the onion and garlic. Raise heat to medium-high and cook, about 2 minutes, stirring continuously. The mixture will stick to the pot. Gradually add the tomato puree, 1 tablespoon at a time, stirring until all the puree is added. Add the beans, lime juice, ½ cup water, and salt. Reduce the heat to low, cover, and simmer for 3 minutes. Top with chopped cilantro. Serve hot.

EACH SERVING PROVIDES

192 calories, 10.4 g protein, 36.6 g carbohydrate

1.5 g fat, 669 mg sodium, 0 mg cholesterol

SERVING SUGGESTION

Serve over a bed of rice with spicy "stir-fried" potatoes (page 186) and a mixed green salad.

BROCCOLI IN SICHUAN SAUCE

YIELD: 4 SERVINGS

In this preparation, the broccoli retains its rich green color. This dish takes very little time, and it can be prepared at the last moment.

6 cups fresh broccoli florets
2 tablespoons white rice vinegar
2 tablespoons low-sodium soy sauce
2 tablespoons lime juice
$\frac{1}{4}$ cup water
1 teaspoon arrowroot
1 teaspoon garlic powder

Fill a 4-quart stainless steel pot with 3 quarts of water, cover, and bring to a boil over high heat. Uncover, reduce heat to medium, and add a single layer of florets. Cook for 3 minutes or until crisp-tender; transfer to a colander with slotted spoon or tongs. Repeat until all of the broccoli has been blanched. Set broccoli aside.

In a small stainless steel saucepan, combine the vinegar, soy sauce, lime juice, water, arrowroot, and garlic powder and cook on low heat until it begins to thicken, which should only take 1 minute. Immediately pour it over the cooked broccoli and toss gently to coat the florets. Serve hot.

EACH SERVING PROVIDES
47 calories, 4.5 g protein, 9.5 g carbohydrate
0.5 g fat, 350 mg sodium, 0 mg cholesterol

SERVING SUGGESTION

Serve with Oriental rice "stir-fry" (page 224) and a baked potato.

CABBAGE AND PEAS "STIR-FRY"

YIELD: 5 SERVINGS

This recipe and all its variations can make any vegetable delicious. The trick is in adding the right blend of spices.

¼ teaspoon black mustard seeds or caraway seeds
1 teaspoon ground cumin
½ teaspoon ground coriander
½ teaspoon turmeric
2 tablespoons processed onion
1 tablespoon processed garlic
½ head medium-size green cabbage, sliced, washed, and drained
1 cup frozen peas
Cayenne to taste
Salt to taste
Lemon juice to taste
1 tablespoon fresh chopped cilantro or parsley

Place a large nonstick or stainless steel saucepan, wok, or deep-frying pan on medium heat for 1 minute. Add the mustard seeds and cook until they begin to pop, about 1½ minutes. Immediately add the cumin, coriander, and turmeric and stir for 1 minute. Add the onion and garlic and stir on medium heat for about 3 minutes. Add the cabbage, peas, cayenne, and salt and stir constantly to ensure the spices are well mixed and the cabbage is slightly cooked yet crisp, about 7 minutes. (Most of the water from the vegetables should have evaporated.) Turn off the heat. Add the lemon juice and mix well. Sprinkle chopped cilantro on top. Serve hot.

EACH SERVING PROVIDES
64 calories, 3.4 g protein, 13.4 g carbohydrate
0.5 g fat, 49 mg sodium, 0 mg cholesterol

SERVING SUGGESTION

This dish goes well with white rice and savory chickpeas (page 134). It can also be used as a stuffing inside pita bread with chopped tomatoes.

RED CABBAGE WITH RED ONION

YIELD: 6 SERVINGS

The lively flavor of red onion fuses with red cabbage in this appetizing stir-fry. To prevent the cabbage from being overdone, be sure to cook it uncovered on medium heat. Fresh hot green chili peppers may be substituted for the red ones.

2 cups sliced red onion
1 teaspoon processed garlic
2 dried red hot chili peppers, sliced in half
6 cups sliced red cabbage
Salt to taste
3 tablespoons lemon juice or to taste

Place the onion and garlic in a 6-quart nonstick saucepan. Turn on the heat to medium-high and cook, stirring for 1½ minutes or until the edges of the onion begin to brown. Add the chili peppers, cabbage, and salt. Reduce heat to medium and cook, stirring frequently, about 8 minutes or until the cabbage is just cooked. Mix in the lemon juice. Serve hot.

EACH SERVING PROVIDES
57 calories, 2.4 g protein, 13.0 g carbohydrate
0.4 g fat, 10 mg sodium, 0 mg cholesterol

SERVING SUGGESTION

Serve with yellow split peas in hot curry paste (page 178) and spinach flat bread (page 210) or rice for a balanced vegetarian menu.

Vegetarian Dishes

CAULIFLOWER WITH GINGER AND GARLIC

YIELD: 4 SERVINGS

Cauliflower tends to need spices to bring out its taste, and this recipe does just that. For variation, a cup of frozen peas may be added with the cauliflower. More cayenne and fresh hot green chili peppers can be added for those who like it hot.

1 medium head fresh cauliflower, cut into florets, or 8 cups cauliflower florets
1 heaping teaspoon chili powder
1 heaping teaspoon paprika
1 teaspoon processed ginger
1 teaspoon processed garlic
Cayenne to taste
Fresh hot green chili pepper to taste, sliced
Salt and black pepper to taste
Lemon juice to taste

Wash and drain the cauliflower and set aside. Place a 6-quart stainless steel saucepan on medium-high heat. Add the chili powder and paprika and cook, 1 minute or until the spices begin to roast. Immediately reduce heat to low, add ginger and garlic, and stir a few seconds. Add the cauliflower, cayenne, chili pepper, salt, and black pepper. Cover and cook on low heat, about 25 minutes or until the cauliflower is just done. Raise the heat to high and stir briskly to reduce the juice. Add the lemon juice. Serve hot.

EACH SERVING PROVIDES
55 calories, 4.3 g protein, 11.3 g carbohydrate
0.6 g fat, 37 mg sodium, 0 mg cholesterol

SERVING SUGGESTION

Serve with gourmet black-eyed peas (page 124), cucumber yogurt relish (page 248), and rice for a complete meal.

SAVORY CHICKPEAS

YIELD: 4 SERVINGS

Canned chickpeas are convenient and work well for this delicious and protein-rich vegetarian preparation. Rinsing and draining the chickpeas reduces the content of salt and preservatives. Be sure to have all ingredients measured and on hand before you start cooking.

1 teaspoon ground cumin
½ teaspoon ground coriander
½ teaspoon turmeric
4 heaping tablespoons processed onion
1 teaspoon processed garlic
4 tablespoons tomato puree
2 (15-ounce) cans chickpeas, rinsed and drained
Salt to taste
Cayenne to taste
3 slices tomato

Place a 4-quart stainless steel saucepan on medium-high heat. Add the cumin, coriander, and turmeric and stir for 1 minute to dry-roast. Look for a slight amount of smoke rising from the pot. The turmeric will turn an orange-brown shade, but do not let the spices blacken. If they do, set aside to cool, discard, and start again.

Add the onion and garlic and stir (the mixture may stick due to lack of oil). Lower heat to ensure it does not burn. Gradually add the tomato puree, raise heat to medium, and stir for 4 minutes (a few drops of water may be added while stirring to prevent sticking). Add the chickpeas, salt, cayenne, and 1 cup water. Cover and simmer for 8 to 10 minutes on low heat (the water may be increased or decreased, depending on the consistency of gravy preferred). Remove chickpeas to serving dish and garnish with tomato slices. Serve.

EACH SERVING PROVIDES
253 calories, 10.3 g protein, 49.2 g carbohydrate
2.4 g fat, 427 mg sodium, 0 mg cholesterol

SERVING SUGGESTION

Serve on a bed of rice-vegetable pilaf (page 226), or plain rice, with spicy mixed vegetables (page 196) and tangy green cilantro chutney (page 232).

MOROCCAN COUSCOUS WITH VEGETABLES

YIELD: 4 SERVINGS

Couscous, a staple grain of Morocco, is quickly gaining popularity as an alternative to rice and breads. This spicy version tastes more like a couscous pilaf, with mixed vegetables and herbs. If you wish, cumin seeds can replace the mustard seeds and parsley can replace the cilantro.

1 teaspoon black mustard seeds or cumin seeds
½ teaspoon ground cumin
½ teaspoon ground coriander
1 teaspoon turmeric
1 cup finely diced onion
1 fresh hot green chili pepper, finely chopped
1 cup frozen peas
1 cup fresh or frozen diced carrots
1 cup couscous
Salt to taste
2 tablespoons chopped cilantro leaves
2 tablespoons lime juice or to taste

Place a 4-quart or larger stainless steel saucepan on medium-high heat. Add the mustard seeds, cover with a lid, and wait until you hear the seeds begin to pop. Reduce heat to low, uncover, and immediately add the cumin, coriander, and turmeric. Stir for a few seconds to roast the ground spices. Add the onion and chili pepper and stir for 1 minute. Add the peas, carrots, couscous, 2½ cups water, and salt. Stir well, cover, and cook on low heat for 20 minutes or until the couscous has absorbed the water. Mix in the cilantro and lime juice. Fluff the couscous gently with a fork. Serve hot.

EACH SERVING PROVIDES
251 calories, 9.4 g protein, 51.4 g carbohydrate
0.9 g fat, 81 mg sodium, 0 mg cholesterol

SERVING SUGGESTION
Serve with "creamed" spinach (page 138) and mixed greens for a balanced vegetarian meal.

"CREAMED" SPINACH

YIELD: 3 SERVINGS

For spinach lovers, this is a simple, quick, and delicious side dish. Spinach complements any meat, fish, or vegetarian meal. The creamy texture comes from the evaporated skim milk; however, for individuals wishing to avoid dairy products, ¼ cup tomato puree may replace the milk.

1 (10-ounce) box frozen chopped spinach, thawed
½ cup canned evaporated skim milk
2 heaping tablespoons processed onion
1 teaspoon processed garlic
Salt to taste

Place the spinach and skim milk in a food processor and process to a smooth puree. Place a 3-quart stainless steel saucepan on medium-high heat. Add the onion and garlic and stir well, about 3 minutes. This mixture will tend to stick due to lack of oil; adjust heat accordingly and scrape the bottom of the pot occasionally. Add the spinach and salt and continue stirring well, about 3 minutes. Lower heat, cover, and simmer, about 8 minutes. Uncover, raise the heat, and cook, 3 to 4 minutes, until juice from the spinach evaporates. Serve hot.

EACH SERVING PROVIDES
79 calories, 6.9 g protein, 14.1 g carbohydrate
0.4 g fat, 133 mg sodium, 2 mg cholesterol

SERVING SUGGESTION

Serve with vegetarian "ground meat" with peas (page 156) and elegant rice with mushrooms (page 220).

SPINACH AND CHEESE ENCHILADAS WITH HOMEMADE SALSA

YIELD: 2 SERVINGS

This savory dish from South of the Border can be customized to your taste. Make it mild or fiery, with various tasty fillings and toppings. Here, the traditional bean and meat filling has been replaced by spinach and fat-free ricotta. Homemade salsa is easy to make; substitute ½ cup chopped green bell pepper in place of jalapeño for a milder salsa.

Homemade Salsa
1 cup canned tomatoes, drained
1 medium onion, sliced, rinsed, and drained
1 to 2 jalapeño peppers, finely sliced
1 tablespoon distilled white vinegar
Salt to taste

The Enchiladas
1 teaspoon ground cumin
1 teaspoon processed garlic
1 (10-ounce) box frozen chopped spinach, thawed
1 cup fat-free ricotta cheese
Salt and pepper to taste
4 fat-free flour tortillas (8 inches in diameter)
Nonstick cooking spray

To make the salsa, combine all the salsa ingredients in a food processor; process for 30 seconds, until

Vegetarian Dishes

vegetables are finely chopped. Do not overprocess. Adjust seasoning to taste. (Any leftover salsa can be refrigerated for one week in an airtight jar.)

To make the enchiladas, place a 3-quart stainless steel saucepan on medium heat. Add the cumin and stir for 1 minute. Add the garlic, spinach, ricotta, salt, and pepper. Cook on high heat, stirring continuously, until the liquid has more or less evaporated from the ricotta-spinach mixture. This will take about 8 minutes. Set aside.

Warm tortillas according to package directions and keep covered. Lightly spray a microwave-safe dish large enough to hold the tortillas with nonstick cooking spray. Divide the spinach mixture evenly and spoon onto each tortilla. Roll up the tortillas and place them on the dish, seam-side down. Cover lightly with a paper towel and microwave on high, about 2 minutes or until piping hot. Alternatively, preheat oven to 400 degrees F, wrap enchiladas individually in foil, and bake for 20 minutes. Top hot enchiladas with salsa and serve immediately.

EACH SERVING PROVIDES
378 calories, 30.4 g protein, 73.2 g carbohydrate
2.1 g fat, 959 mg sodium, 20 mg cholesterol

SERVING SUGGESTION
Serve with mixed greens, chopped tomatoes, and mock guacamole (page 236) for a Mexican treat.

ATHENIAN EGGPLANT WITH HERBS

YIELD: 4 SERVINGS

The lively charm of the Greek people is reflected in their cuisine. Vegetables are prepared in various imaginative ways, and this version of eggplant is commonly served in many restaurants in Athens.

1 medium eggplant, peeled and sliced into
    1-inch pieces (about 6 cups)
Nonstick cooking spray
2 large scallions, finely sliced (green ends included)
1 teaspoon processed garlic
½ teaspoon ground nutmeg
3 tablespoons fresh chopped parsley
3 tablespoons fresh chopped dill
2 tablespoons lemon juice
2 tablespoons tomato puree
2 heaping tablespoons fat-free or lowfat
    bread crumbs
Salt and pepper to taste
Dill sprigs

Place eggplant in a microwave-safe dish, cover, and microwave on high until softened, about 8 to 10 minutes (rotate the dish twice in that time). Alternatively, place eggplant with 2 tablespoons of water in a nonstick pan, cover, and cook on low heat for 30 minutes. Transfer the eggplant to a food processor and process to a puree. Set aside. Place a

10-inch nonstick skillet on medium-high heat and spray lightly with nonstick cooking spray. Add the scallions and garlic and cook for 2 minutes. Reduce the heat to low and add the eggplant, nutmeg, parsley, dill, lemon juice, tomato puree, and bread crumbs. Season with salt and pepper and stir all ingredients well. Cover and cook on low heat for 5 minutes. Garnish with sprigs of fresh dill. Serve hot or at room temperature.

EACH SERVING PROVIDES
48 calories, 1.8 g protein, 10.4 g carbohydrate
0.5 g fat, 40 mg sodium, 0 mg cholesterol

SERVING SUGGESTION

Serve as an appetizer with warmed whole wheat pita or as a side vegetable in place of mashed potatoes.

SPICY EGGPLANT

YIELD: 4 SERVINGS

This is an excellent vegetarian preparation to be served on the side with any meal.

1 medium eggplant, peeled and sliced into
   1-inch-thick pieces (about 6 cups)
1 teaspoon ground cumin
3 heaping tablespoons processed onion
1 teaspoon processed garlic
1 teaspoon processed or peeled and grated ginger
4 fresh or canned tomatoes, finely diced
1 fresh hot green chili pepper, chopped
1 cup diced green bell pepper
Salt to taste
2 tablespoons lemon juice
1 cup finely chopped fresh cilantro

Place the eggplant in a microwave-safe bowl, cover, and microwave until tender, about 8 minutes (rotate the dish twice in that time). Alternatively, place eggplant with 2 tablespoons of water in a non-stick pan, cover, and cook on low heat for 30 minutes. Set aside to cool.

Transfer the cooled eggplant to a food processor and process to a puree. Heat a 4-quart stainless steel saucepan on medium-high heat, add the cumin, and stir for 40 seconds. Add the onion, garlic, and ginger. Lower the heat if the ingredients begin to burn, adding tomatoes gradually to prevent the mixture from sticking to the saucepan; cook 3 minutes on medium heat, stirring continuously. Stir in chili pepper, eggplant puree, green pepper, and salt. Cover and cook on low heat for 4 minutes. Adjust seasoning if necessary and add lemon juice and cilantro. Mix well. Serve hot.

EACH SERVING PROVIDES
95 calories, 3.7 g protein, 21.2 g carbohydrate
0.8 g fat, 26 mg sodium, 0 mg cholesterol

SERVING SUGGESTION

Serve with warm spinach flat bread (page 210) and savory chickpeas (page 134) for a complete meal.

EGGPLANT AND CARROTS WITH FENNEL

YIELD: 6 SERVINGS

Fennel seeds and a dash of lemon juice give this
eggplant dish its distinctive flavor. Carrots add
their own taste and texture. Be sure to have all
ingredients measured and on hand before you
start cooking.

½ teaspoon cumin seeds
½ teaspoon fennel seeds
½ teaspoon ground cumin
½ teaspoon ground coriander
½ teaspoon turmeric
3 heaping tablespoons processed onion
1 tablespoon processed garlic
1 medium eggplant, washed and sliced into
    ½-inch pieces (about 6 cups)
1 large carrot, peeled and sliced into
    ¼-inch-thick rounds
1 hot green chili pepper, seeded and
    finely chopped
Salt to taste
Lemon juice to taste
1 tablespoon chopped fresh cilantro

Place a 6-quart stainless steel saucepan on medium-
high heat. Add the cumin seeds and fennel seeds
and stir for 1 minute until the seeds begin to pop.

Reduce the heat to low and add the ground cumin, coriander, and turmeric and stir, about 1 minute. Add the onion and garlic. Increase the heat to medium and stir constantly for 2 minutes (the mixture will tend to stick; scrape the bottom occasionally). Add the eggplant, carrot, chili pepper, and salt. Cover, lower heat, and cook until vegetables are tender, about 20 minutes. Stir in lemon juice and cilantro. Transfer to serving dish and serve hot.

EACH SERVING PROVIDES
48 calories, 1.8 g protein, 10.9 g carbohydrate
0.3 g fat, 10 mg sodium, 0 mg cholesterol

SERVING SUGGESTION

Spinach flat bread (page 210) or pita bread and gourmet black-eyed peas (page 124) complement this dish nicely.

VEGETARIAN FAJITAS

YIELD: 2 SERVINGS

Warmed tortillas are stuffed with seasoned tofu strips and vegetables in this Mexican vegetarian entree. You'll find lowfat tofu in some supermarkets and Asian markets.

2 tablespoons low-sodium soy sauce
2 tablespoons red wine vinegar
¼ pound extra-firm lowfat tofu, drained, cut into sticks, 2 inches by 1 inch by ⅛ inch
½ teaspoon ground cumin
½ teaspoon processed garlic
2 medium onions, finely sliced
1 cup sliced red bell pepper (1½-inch sticks)
1 cup sliced green bell pepper (1½-inch sticks)
2 tablespoons frozen cut corn
Salt to taste
2 tablespoons chopped cilantro leaves
4 fat-free flour tortillas (9 inches in diameter)

Combine the soy sauce and vinegar in a bowl and marinate the tofu pieces for 5 minutes. Place a 5-quart nonstick saucepan or frying pan on high heat. Add the cumin and cook for 40 seconds. Add the garlic, onions, red and green pepper, corn, and salt. Cook on low heat, 6 to 8 minutes or until vegetables are crisp-tender, stirring occasionally. Add the tofu and the marinade. Increase the heat to medium-high and cook until most of the marinade evaporates. Turn off the heat, mix in the cilantro, and set aside.

Warm the tortillas according to package directions. Fill the tortillas with the vegetable-tofu mixture, roll, and place seam side down on a serving dish. Serve hot.

EACH SERVING PROVIDES

310 calories, 14.3 g protein, 70.0 g carbohydrate
2.2 g fat, 1060 mg sodium, 0 mg cholesterol

SERVING SUGGESTION

Serve with jalapeño dip (page 238) and mock guacamole (page 236).

HASH BROWNS

YIELD: 3 SERVINGS

A no-fuss alternative to eggs or an addition to a leisurely weekend brunch, this dish can be made in minutes with very basic ingredients.

2 tablespoons finely chopped parsley
2 tablespoons cornmeal flour
1 tablespoon all-purpose flour
1 cup peeled and coarsely grated potatoes
$\frac{1}{3}$ cup finely diced onion, rinsed and drained
Salt and pepper to taste
$\frac{1}{2}$ teaspoon dried thyme
1 tablespoon lemon juice
Nonstick cooking spray

In a bowl, mix the parsley, flours, potatoes, onion, salt, pepper, thyme, lemon juice, and 1 tablespoon water. Shape the mixture into $1\frac{1}{2}$-inch round or oblong patties and set aside. Place a nonstick pan or skillet on medium-high heat. When hot, spray evenly with nonstick cooking spray and place the patties into the pan. Let the mixture set and brown on one side. Flip over gently, flatten with a spatula, and brown the other side. Lower heat, cover, and cook until potatoes are tender, about 8 minutes. Serve.

EACH SERVING PROVIDES
87 calories, 2.0 g protein, 19.2 g carbohydrate
0.3 g fat, 4 mg sodium, 0 mg cholesterol

SERVING SUGGESTION

Top with hot sauce or ketchup and serve for breakfast with vegetarian scramble (page 204) and toast.

VEGETABLE LO MEIN

YIELD: 4 SERVINGS

The vegetables for this dish can be substituted with any that you have on hand. Vegetables such as snow peas, water chestnuts, bok choy, and mushrooms are a good choice, and broccoli and carrots add color.

1 cup carrot sticks (1 inch long)
1 cup frozen cut green beans
1 cup frozen cut broccoli
Nonstick cooking spray
4 scallions, finely sliced (green ends included)
1 teaspoon garlic powder
2 cups cooked spaghetti or linguine
2 tablespoons white rice vinegar
2 tablespoons water
½ teaspoon arrowroot
3 tablespoons low-sodium soy sauce
Dash Tabasco sauce or hot sauce

In a microwave-safe dish, combine the carrots, green beans, and broccoli, microwave on high for about 4 minutes or until crisp-tender; drain. Alternatively, place the carrots, green beans, broccoli, and ¼ cup water in a 3-quart stainless steel pot, cover, cook on low heat for 20 minutes; drain.

Set a 6-quart nonstick pot on medium heat. Add the scallions and sauté for 1½ minutes. Add the garlic powder and stir for 30 seconds. Add the vegetables and spaghetti. Toss well until the ingredients are heated through, cover, and set aside.

In a small stainless steel saucepan, combine the vinegar, water, arrowroot, and soy sauce and cook on medium heat until the sauce begins to thicken. Immediately pour the sauce over the noodles and mix well. Serve hot, with Tabasco sauce.

EACH SERVING PROVIDES
154 calories, 6.7 g protein, 31.8 g carbohydrate
0.8 g fat, 497 mg sodium, 0 mg cholesterol

SERVING SUGGESTION

Serve as a meal in itself or as a side dish with savory stuffed potatoes (page 188) and a green salad.

MACARONI VEGETABLE MIX-UP

YIELD: 2 SERVINGS

This side dish of pasta and vegetables makes good use of any frozen or odd pieces of fresh vegetables you may have on hand.

1 cup sliced onion
½ teaspoon garlic powder
2 tablespoons low-sodium soy sauce or to taste
3 carrots, peeled, diced, and cooked until crisp-tender
1 cup frozen peas, thawed and drained
1 cup shredded cabbage
1 cup fresh mushrooms, washed and sliced
1 cup cooked macaroni or any small-size pasta
Dash hot sauce (optional)

Place a 5-quart nonstick saucepan on medium-high heat. Add the onion and sauté for 2 minutes. Add the garlic powder, soy sauce, carrots, peas, cabbage, and mushrooms and sauté, 2 to 3 minutes. Add the cooked macaroni and stir for 1 minute. Add the hot sauce, if using, mix well, and serve immediately.

EACH SERVING PROVIDES

268 calories, 11.7 g protein, 54.7 g carbohydrate

1.3 g fat, 721 mg sodium, 0 mg cholesterol

SERVING SUGGESTION

This dish goes well with bean and potato patties (page 176) topped with tangy green cilantro chutney (page 232).

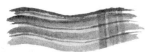

VEGETARIAN "GROUND MEAT" WITH PEAS

YIELD: 4 SERVINGS

The chewy texture of processed mushrooms makes it a vegetarian substitute for ground meat. Have all ingredients measured and on hand, since this is a quick process. If the recipe is doubled, the cooking time will increase accordingly.

6 ounces fresh white mushrooms
1 teaspoon ground cumin
1 teaspoon ground coriander
1 teaspoon turmeric
1 teaspoon processed garlic
2 tablespoons processed onion
2 tablespoons nonfat plain yogurt
4 tablespoons tomato puree
1½ cups frozen peas
Salt to taste
½ cup water

Wash, drain, and cut the mushrooms in quarters. Process mushrooms in a food processor by pressing the Pulse button 5 to 6 times to obtain a "chopped" consistency; do not overprocess. Set aside.

Place a 4-quart stainless steel saucepan on medium heat. Add the cumin, coriander, and turmeric and stir, about 1 minute, until slightly roasted (a small amount of smoke in the pot is a good indication of this). Immediately add the garlic and onion and cook on medium heat for about 9 minutes, stirring constantly (the mixture will tend to stick). Gradually add the yogurt and tomato puree and lower the heat, if necessary, to prevent burning. Add the mushrooms, peas, salt, and water. Cover and simmer for 4 minutes. Serve hot.

EACH SERVING PROVIDES
88 calories, 5.3 g protein, 16.6 g carbohydrate
0.7 g fat, 120 mg sodium, 0 mg cholesterol

SERVING SUGGESTION

Serve with rice, warm whole wheat pita, or garlic toast (page 214) and mixed sprout salad (page 54).

FRENCH-STYLE "CREAMED" MUSHROOMS

YIELD: 4 SERVINGS

Even though French food is traditionally associated with rich sauces, in this French favorite butter is eliminated in the sauce and the flour is lightly roasted before adding the milk and the right blend of herbs. Serve it on the side for breakfast, lunch, or dinner. This dish, which freezes and microwaves very well, can be made ahead of time. Have all ingredients measured and on hand for easy preparation.

3 tablespoons all-purpose flour
1 cup skim milk
1 pound fresh mushrooms, cleaned and sliced
½ cup finely diced onion, rinsed and drained
½ cup finely diced green bell pepper
¼ teaspoon dried basil
¼ teaspoon dried thyme
Salt and pepper to taste
1 tablespoon grated fat-free cheddar cheese,
     or to taste
Fresh sprigs of dill or parsley

Place a 3-quart stainless steel saucepan on medium heat for 1 minute. Add the flour and stir constantly for 1 minute. Remove from heat and set aside to cool for 5 minutes. Gradually add the milk to the cooled flour, stirring continuously to remove any lumps; if lumps do form, process mixture in a food processor. Return pan to low heat and add the mushrooms, onion, green pepper, basil, thyme, salt, and pepper and stir, 2 minutes. Cover and cook on low heat, 7 minutes or until mushrooms and peppers are tender. Mix in the cheese and stir until melted. This dish should have a thick, creamy consistency. If it is too thick, add a little more milk and cook for 1 minute. If the consistency is too thin, cook uncovered to reduce the sauce. Garnish with dill or parsley. Serve warm or at room temperature.

EACH SERVING PROVIDES
86 calories, 6.0 g protein, 15.4 g carbohydrate
0.7 g fat, 47 mg sodium, 1 mg cholesterol

SERVING SUGGESTION

Serve on melba toast or crackers for an interesting appetizer.

BUTTON MUSHROOMS IN TOMATO SAUCE

YIELD: 3 SERVINGS

If button mushrooms are not available, any type of mushroom may be cut in halves or thirds for this recipe. The fennel gives this dish a subtle licorice flavor.

4 cups button mushrooms
½ teaspoon ground coriander
½ teaspoon finely ground fennel seeds
2 bay leaves
¼ teaspoon dried thyme
1 heaping tablespoon processed onion
4 tablespoons tomato puree
Salt and pepper to taste
Chopped parsley

Wash and drain the mushrooms. Place a 5-quart stainless steel saucepan on medium-high heat. Add the coriander, fennel seeds, bay leaves, and thyme and cook for 1½ minutes or until the spices begin to roast. Add the onion and cook for 2 minutes (lower the heat if the mixture begins to burn). Stir in the tomato puree, mushrooms, salt, and pepper. Cover and cook on low heat, about 7 minutes. Discard bay leaves. Garnish with parsley and serve hot.

EACH SERVING PROVIDES
42 calories, 2.6 g protein, 8.5 g carbohydrate
0.6 g fat, 80 mg sodium, 0 mg cholesterol

SERVING SUGGESTION

Serve as a spicy side dish with gourmet black-eyed peas (page 124), spicy potato salad (page 55), and rice.

APPETIZING MUSHROOMS AND PEAS

YIELD: 4 SERVINGS

Mushrooms cooked in any way are wonderful. Despite what the experts recommend about wiping mushrooms instead of washing them, fresh mushrooms do need to be thoroughly rinsed and drained. However, if mushrooms are left soaking in water for more than 20 minutes, they absorb moisture and lose their crisp texture.

12 ounces fresh, whole mushrooms
2 heaping tablespoons processed onion
1 teaspoon processed garlic
Salt and pepper to taste
1 cup frozen peas
1 tablespoon fresh lemon juice

Wash, drain, and slice the mushrooms. Place a 5-quart nonstick saucepan on medium heat. Add the onion and garlic and cook for 2 minutes, stirring continuously (the mixture will stick to the pan). Add the mushrooms, salt, and pepper and stir well. Lower the heat, cover, and cook, 12 to 14 minutes.

Add the peas, raise the heat to medium-high, and cook, uncovered, about 3 minutes or until the peas are cooked and the vegetable juice has more or less been reduced. Sprinkle lemon juice on top and serve hot.

EACH SERVING PROVIDES
68 calories, 4.3 g protein, 13.1 g carbohydrate
0.5 g fat, 38 mg sodium, 0 mg cholesterol

SERVING SUGGESTION

Serve with vegetarian scramble (page 204), spinach flat bread (page 210) or warm whole wheat pita, green salad, and tangy tomato-ginger chutney (page 234).

SPINACH-STUFFED MUSHROOMS

YIELD: 12 STUFFED MUSHROOMS

A good choice for an appetizer or a side dish, this recipe requires large, firm, and unblemished white stuffing mushrooms. Pureed spinach gives a creamy texture to the stuffing.

1 (10-ounce) package frozen chopped spinach, thawed
4 sprigs fresh dill
12 ounces large, fresh mushrooms
2 heaping tablespoons processed onion
1 teaspoon processed garlic
2 tablespoons tomato puree or tomato paste
Salt to taste
1 tablespoon lemon juice or to taste
2 tablespoons fat-free parmesan cheese

Puree the spinach and dill in a food processor. Wash and drain the mushrooms. Gently remove the stems and finely chop them. Set mushrooms caps upside down while you prepare the filling.

In a 4-quart stainless steel saucepan, add the onion and garlic. Set pan over medium-high heat and cook for 3 minutes. Add the spinach, tomato puree, chopped mushroom stems, and salt. Cover and cook on low heat for 5 minutes. Stir in the lemon juice and remove from heat. With a small spoon, fill the hollowed mushrooms caps with the stuffing.

To cook in a microwave, line a microwave-safe baking dish with 2 layers of paper towels. Place the mushrooms in the dish, cover, and cook on high for 5 to 7 minutes or until mushrooms are just softened. To cook in the oven, preheat the oven to 400 degrees F. Place mushrooms in a baking dish covered with foil and bake for 25 minutes. Sprinkle with cheese and serve warm.

EACH MUSHROOM PROVIDES

23 calories, 1.7 g protein, 4.5 g carbohydrate

0.2 g fat, 41 mg sodium, 1 mg cholesterol

SERVING SUGGESTION

Serve with vegetable fritters (page 202), wild rice, yummy baked beans (page 118), and tomato, cucumber, and onion relish (page 247).

"FRIED" OKRA WITH ONION

YIELD: 4 SERVINGS

This recipe is for okra lovers. Okra, when cooked right, is delicious. The simple rule when buying okra is to make sure that it is tender (tough okra will not cook). Test it by breaking a small piece between your finger and thumb—it should snap easily. Rinse, drain, and allow the okra to dry to ensure that no moisture is present. Not a drop of water should be added during the entire cooking process, and this vegetable should be cooked uncovered, because the slightest buildup of steam causes the okra to emit a sticky substance.

½ pound fresh okra, rinsed, drained, and allowed
   to dry
Nonstick cooking spray
2 cups sliced onion
1 teaspoon turmeric
Salt to taste

Cut away the knobby heads of the okra and discard. Slice the okra across into ⅛-inch-thick round slices.

Place a 12-inch nonstick frying pan on medium-high heat. When hot, spray the pan lightly with nonstick cooking spray, add the onion, and sauté for

2 minutes. Stir in the turmeric. Add the okra and salt, lower heat slightly, and cook uncovered for 8 to 10 minutes or until the okra is just tender, shaking the pan occasionally. Handle gently. The sticky substance, which will be visible during cooking, will disappear by the time the okra is cooked. Serve hot.

EACH SERVING PROVIDES
58 calories, 2.3 g protein, 12.4 g carbohydrate
0.4 g fat, 4 mg sodium, 0 mg cholesterol

SERVING SUGGESTION

Serve with savory chickpeas (page 134), green salad, spicy "stir-fried" potatoes (page 186), and spinach flat bread (page 210).

PENNE PASTA WITH BASIL-MUSHROOM SAUCE

YIELD: 2 SERVINGS

Fresh parsley may replace basil in this zesty sauce, which can be served over any pasta you like.

2 cups crushed tomatoes
1 cup sliced fresh mushrooms
½ cup chopped fresh basil
1 teaspoon processed garlic
2 tablespoons processed onion
½ teaspoon dried oregano
2 tablespoons red wine vinegar
Salt and pepper to taste
2 cups cooked penne pasta, rinsed and drained
Fat-free parmesan cheese to taste
Fresh sprigs of basil

In a 3-quart stainless steel saucepan, mix the tomatoes, mushrooms, basil, garlic, onion, oregano, vinegar, salt, and pepper, cover, and simmer on low heat for 8 minutes. Pour the sauce over the pasta, sprinkle with cheese, and garnish with basil. Serve hot.

EACH SERVING PROVIDES
286 calories, 10.9 g protein, 59.4 g carbohydrate
1.9 g fat, 393 mg sodium, 0 mg cholesterol

SERVING SUGGESTION

Serve with asparagus-mushroom crostini (page 212) and savory stuffed potatoes (page 188).

TRI-PEPPER PASTA

YIELD: 4 SERVINGS

A colorful medley of peppers, onion, and tomatoes are tossed with pasta for a tasty side dish. Onions can be easily "browned" in a little soy sauce.

3 tablespoons red wine vinegar
2 tablespoons lime juice
1 tablespoon low-sodium soy sauce
1 teaspoon processed garlic
1 cup finely sliced onion
1 cup sliced red bell pepper (1-inch sticks)
1 cup sliced green bell pepper (1-inch sticks)
1 cup sliced yellow bell pepper (1-inch sticks)
2 cups cooked ziti or penne pasta
1 cup chopped fresh tomatoes
Salt to taste
2 tablespoons chopped fresh basil leaves

In a bowl, combine the vinegar and lime juice and set aside. Heat a 6-quart stainless steel pot on medium-high heat and add the soy sauce. Add the garlic and onion and cook for 1 minute. Reduce the heat to low, add the red, green, and yellow peppers, cover, and cook for 4 minutes. Add the pasta, lime-vinegar mixture, tomatoes, and salt. Raise the heat to medium-high and cook briskly for 1 minute. Remove to serving dish and top with fresh basil. Serve hot.

EACH SERVING PROVIDES
150 calories, 5.2 g protein, 32.1 g carbohydrate
0.8 g fat, 157 mg sodium, 0 mg cholesterol

SERVING SUGGESTION

Garlic toast (page 214) and cold mushroom-spinach salad (page 58) go well with this preparation.

POTATO PATTIES STUFFED WITH PEAS

YIELD: 6 TO 7 PATTIES

Spicy pea stuffing makes this an interesting side dish.

Stuffing
½ teaspoon cumin seeds
1 heaping tablespoon processed onion
1½ cups frozen peas
Salt to taste
½ cup chopped fresh cilantro
2 tablespoons lemon juice

Potato Patties
10 small potatoes, boiled, peeled, and mashed
    (about 2½ cups)
2 fresh hot green chili peppers, finely diced
4 tablespoons lemon juice
1 teaspoon ground cumin
1 teaspoon ground coriander
1 teaspoon chili powder
Salt to taste
⅓ cup cornmeal flour
Nonstick cooking spray

To make the stuffing, place a 3-quart stainless steel saucepan on medium-high heat and add the cumin seeds; cook for 1 minute or until they begin to pop. Add the onion and cook on low to medium heat for 2 minutes, stirring continuously. Add the peas and salt, cover, and cook on low heat for 5 minutes or until peas are tender. Remove from heat, mix in cilantro and lemon juice, and set aside.

To make the patties, in a bowl, mix the potatoes, chili peppers, lemon juice, cumin, coriander, chili powder, and salt. Adjust seasoning and lemon juice if necessary. Measure 2 tablespoons of the potato mixture and shape into a patty. Make a dent in the middle of a patty and fill with about 1 teaspoon of the pea stuffing; cover with more potato mixture to form a smooth patty. Repeat with remaining mixture to form 6 to 7 patties. (Handle gently, as they tend to break.) Dust each patty lightly with cornmeal flour.

Set a 12-inch nonstick frying pan over medium-high heat. Spray with nonstick cooking spray and add as many patties as will fit without crowding. Brown patties lightly on both sides. To prevent breakage, use two implements to turn patties over. Place finished patties on a warm plate while the rest are cooking. Serve warm.

EACH PATTY PROVIDES
162 calories, 4.8 g protein, 34.9 g carbohydrate
0.8 g fat, 42 mg sodium, 0 mg cholesterol

SERVING SUGGESTION

Serve as a side dish or on a toasted bun with jalapeño dip (page 238) or tangy green cilantro chutney (page 232), or serve as a stuffing inside pita bread with shredded lettuce and chopped tomato.

Vegetarian Dishes

VEGETABLE PATTIES

YIELD: 20 PATTIES

Frozen vegetables work well in this vegetarian preparation, which can be served for breakfast, lunch, dinner, or a healthy snack (they can also be made into cocktail-size appetizers). Use less chili peppers if you prefer a milder flavor. If the patty mixture is too moist to handle, mix in a crumbled slice of white bread or 1 tablespoon lowfat bread crumbs to soak up the excess moisture.

½ cup cooked peas, drained
1 cup cooked green beans, drained
1 cup cooked broccoli, drained
1 cup cooked carrot slices, drained
1 cup peeled and chopped onion, rinsed
　　and drained
1 teaspoon processed garlic
1 teaspoon ground cumin
1 teaspoon ground coriander
Salt to taste
Juice of 1 lemon
½ cup fresh cilantro leaves
Cayenne to taste
2 fresh hot green chili peppers
1 cup boiled, peeled, and mashed potatoes
½ cup cornmeal flour
Nonstick cooking spray

Put the peas, beans, broccoli, carrot, onion, garlic, cumin, coriander, salt, lemon juice, cilantro, cayenne, and chili peppers in a food processor and puree to a paste. In a bowl, combine the vegetable mixture and potatoes. Adjust lemon juice, salt, and spices to taste. Shape the mixture into patties, about 2 inches in diameter and ¼ inch thick. Coat with cornmeal flour.

Place a nonstick frying pan or skillet on medium-high heat. When hot, spray evenly with nonstick cooking spray and carefully place a few patties at a time in the pan. Brown on both sides. Since the patties tend to break easily when flipping over, use a fork to lift the patty and a spatula to gently turn it over. Serve hot.

EACH PATTY PROVIDES
44 calories, 1.5 g protein, 9.5 g carbohydrate
0.2 g fat, 14 mg sodium, 0 mg cholesterol

SERVING SUGGESTION

The patties taste good in sandwiches, stuffed inside pita bread, or served on toast, topped with lettuce, tomato, and jalapeño dip (page 238) or tangy green cilantro chutney (page 232).

BEAN AND POTATO PATTIES

YIELD: 12 PATTIES

This protein-rich vegetarian patty is an excellent alternative to burgers. Any variety of canned beans can be used.

1 cup canned pink, red, or pinto beans,
   rinsed and drained
½ teaspoon processed garlic
½ cup chopped onion, rinsed and drained
¼ teaspoon ground cinnamon
¼ teaspoon ground nutmeg
½ teaspoon dried thyme
1 teaspoon chili powder
5 tablespoons lemon juice
½ cup chopped fresh cilantro
Salt and pepper to taste
1 large potato, boiled, peeled, and mashed
½ cup cornmeal flour
Nonstick cooking spray

Put the beans, garlic, onion, cinnamon, nutmeg, thyme, chili powder, lemon juice, cilantro, salt, and pepper in a food processor and process until well mixed. In a bowl, combine the bean mixture with the mashed potatoes. Adjust seasoning, lemon juice, and spices to taste. Shape the mixture into patties, 2 inches in diameter. Coat with cornmeal flour.

Heat a nonstick pan on medium-high heat and spray evenly with nonstick cooking spray. Add a few patties at a time to the pan and lightly brown on both sides. Serve hot.

EACH PATTY PROVIDES
56 calories, 2.0 g protein, 11.5 g carbohydrate
0.3 g fat, 53 mg sodium, 0 mg cholesterol

SERVING SUGGESTION

Serve as a vegetarian sandwich filling, a stuffing for pita pockets along with shredded lettuce and tomato, or as a side dish with tangy green cilantro chutney (page 232) or hot sauce.

YELLOW SPLIT PEAS IN HOT CURRY PASTE

YIELD: 10 SERVINGS

Split peas are a very inexpensive source of protein and fiber. In this preparation, the hot and spicy curry paste adds its own flavor, and the dish goes especially well over rice. Cut down on the cooking time by soaking the peas overnight.

1 (16-ounce) package dry yellow split peas
1 medium onion, cut into large pieces
3 cloves garlic
2 fresh jalapeño peppers or hot green chili peppers, sliced
3 tablespoons tomato paste
1 (1-inch) piece ginger, peeled and cut
1 teaspoon cumin seeds
1 teaspoon ground cumin
½ teaspoon ground clove
1 teaspoon turmeric
Salt to taste
4 tablespoons lime juice
3 tablespoons chopped cilantro leaves

The night before cooking, pick peas for stones and soak peas in 5 cups of water overnight. Drain, rinse, and cook peas in 6 cups of water for 35 to 40 minutes or until tender. Combine onion, garlic, chili pepper, tomato paste, and ginger in a food processor and process to a paste.

Place a 6-quart stainless steel pot on medium-high heat, add cumin seeds, and stir for 1 minute or until they begin to pop. Lower heat, add ground cumin, clove, and turmeric, and stir for about 40 seconds. Add the processed paste, raise heat, and cook, about 4 minutes, stirring to prevent sticking. (If the mixture sticks, lower heat, add 1 tablespoon water and continue stirring.) Add peas, salt, lime juice, and ½ cup water (you may need to add more or less water, to form a thick, yet soupy consistency). Cover and simmer on low heat for 4 minutes. Top with cilantro and serve hot.

EACH SERVING PROVIDES
179 calories, 12.0 g protein, 32.7 g carbohydrate
0.8 g fat, 49 mg sodium, 0 mg cholesterol

SERVING SUGGESTION

Serve over a bed of rice or with warmed whole wheat pita and spicy mixed vegetables (page 196).

ARABIC-STYLE LENTILS WITH SCALLIONS AND RICE

YIELD: 4 SERVINGS

Scallions, clove, and cinnamon add flavor to this spicy Arabic preparation. To soften lentils, soak them in water overnight. If you are short on time, they can be soaked for only two hours, but that is not ideal. The longer they soak, the faster they will cook.

½ cup dry lentils, soaked a minimum of 2 hours in
    5 cups water
½ cup basmati rice
¼ teaspoon ground clove
½ teaspoon ground cinnamon
1 heaping teaspoon processed garlic
6 scallions, finely sliced (green ends included)
Salt to taste

Drain lentils and set aside in a bowl. Rinse the rice, drain, and set aside in another bowl. Place a 4-quart stainless steel pot on medium-high heat. Add clove and cinnamon, and stir for 30 seconds. Add garlic, scallions, and salt; stir for 1½ minutes. Add lentils and 2 cups water and increase heat to high. After the water has come to a boil, reduce heat to low, cover pot, and simmer for 30 minutes. Add rice, cover, and continue to cook on low heat for 15 minutes. When all of the liquid has been absorbed, remove pot from heat and set aside covered until ready to serve. Serve hot.

EACH SERVING PROVIDES
181 calories, 9.1 g protein, 35.5 g carbohydrate
0.5 g fat, 7 mg sodium, 0 mg cholesterol

SERVING SUGGESTION

Serve with vegetarian "ground meat" with peas (page 156) and cold mushroom-spinach salad (page 58).

STUFFED PEPPERS

YIELD: 8 SERVINGS

Stuffing peppers is a lot easier than it sounds, especially if the potatoes are prepared in advance.

If you are short on time, you can microwave the peppers to reduce the final cooking time. Set unstuffed peppers upside down on a microwave-safe dish lined with a paper towel. Cover peppers with another paper towel and microwave on high, about 4 minutes. The peppers must remain firm, or stuffing them will be difficult. Prepare as instructed; peppers will only need to be cooked for 2 minutes when turned right side up.

This dish is an excellent accompaniment to any dinner menu or buffet.

4 green bell peppers
Spicy "stir-fried" potatoes made with four large
    potatoes (page 186)
Nonstick cooking spray
½ cup whole wheat flour
⅓ cup water
Cilantro, basil, or parsley sprigs

Carefully cut away stems, if any, from the green peppers. Slice green peppers through the middle to form equal halves. Carefully trim the inside edges of the pepper halves with a sharp knife and scoop out the seeds.

In a bowl, mash the potatoes roughly with a fork. Stuff the peppers with the potato mixture all the way above the rim. Gently press the stuffing evenly and firmly using the back of a tablespoon.

Heat a nonstick frying pan or skillet on high heat and spray with nonstick cooking spray. In a separate, small bowl, add the whole wheat flour and gradually mix in water to make a fairly thick, cake-like batter. Pour about 1 tablespoon of this batter evenly over the stuffed pepper and let it spread to cover the top. With a paper towel, wipe any spills down the sides of the pepper. In a quick motion, invert and place each pepper, batter side down, on the hot skillet. Cook for 4 to 5 minutes until the batter is set and golden brown. Turn over and cook the pepper right side up, about 8 minutes, and remove. For garnish, place cilantro, parsley, or basil sprigs on the top of each pepper half. Serve hot.

EACH SERVING PROVIDES
112 calories, 3.1 g protein, 25.2 g carbohydrate
0.6 g fat, 7 mg sodium, 0 mg cholesterol

SERVING SUGGESTION

Serve with button mushrooms in tomato sauce (page 160) and Moroccan couscous with vegetables (page 136).

GOURMET POTATOES AND PEAS

YIELD: 4 SERVINGS

Enjoy this delicious preparation with any menu. Have all ingredients measured and on hand, since the process is quick. The potatoes and peas will have a rich brown gravy; you can adjust the amount of water in this recipe if you prefer more or less gravy.

1 teaspoon ground cumin
½ teaspoon ground coriander
½ teaspoon turmeric
2 heaping tablespoons processed onion
1 teaspoon processed garlic
2 tablespoons tomato puree
2 tablespoons nonfat plain yogurt
1½ cup peeled and diced potatoes
Salt to taste
1 cup water
1 cup frozen peas

Heat a 3-quart stainless steel saucepan on medium-high heat. Add the cumin, coriander, and turmeric and stir, about 2 minutes, to dry-roast (the spices are roasted when there is a very slight amount of smoke coming from the pan). Reduce heat to low, immediately add the onion and garlic, increase the heat to medium-high, and cook, stirring constantly (without oil, this mixture will tend to stick to the bottom of the pan). Gradually stir in the tomato puree and yogurt and cook, about 4 minutes, stirring constantly. Add the potatoes, salt, and water, cover, and cook on low heat, 15 minutes or until the potatoes are tender. Add the peas, cover, and simmer for 5 minutes. Serve warm.

EACH SERVING PROVIDES
110 calories, 4.4 g protein, 22.8 g carbohydrate
0.5 g fat, 86 mg sodium, 0 mg cholesterol

SERVING SUGGESTION
Serve with rice or whole wheat pita, yellow split peas in hot curry paste (page 178), daikon relish (page 246), and lime pickle (page 244).

SPICY "STIR-FRIED" POTATOES

YIELD: 4 SERVINGS

One of the most versatile vegetables, the potato can be made in a hundred different ways. This recipe has a subtle, stir-fry flavor, and it can also be used as a filling for stuffed peppers. Since dry-roasting spices is a quick process, all ingredients should be measured and on hand in this preparation.

You can also boil the potatoes ahead of time, shortening the cooking time to 5 minutes. Add the boiled, peeled, and cubed potatoes after the spices are roasted. Stir all ingredients on low heat until the spices and the potatoes are well mixed and heated through. A tablespoon of water added during stirring will prevent the potatoes from sticking.

2 cups peeled and diced ($\frac{1}{2}$-inch pieces) potatoes
$\frac{1}{2}$ teaspoon whole cumin seeds
1 teaspoon ground cumin
$\frac{1}{2}$ teaspoon ground coriander
$\frac{1}{2}$ teaspoon turmeric
1 tablespoon water
Salt to taste
$\frac{1}{4}$ teaspoon cayenne, or to taste
1 tablespoon fresh lemon juice
1 tablespoon chopped fresh cilantro leaves

Soak the potatoes in cold water to prevent discoloration (drain them just prior to using). Heat a 4-quart stainless steel saucepan on medium-high heat, add the cumin seeds, and stir until they begin to pop, about 1 minute. Reduce the heat immediately to low. Add the ground cumin, coriander, and turmeric and stir for 30 seconds. The spices will smoke, due to the intense heat, but they should not blacken. Immediately stir in the drained potatoes, water, salt, and cayenne, cover, and cook on low heat, about 20 minutes or until the potatoes are tender. If excess liquid remains after the potatoes are cooked, remove the cover, increase the heat, and stir briskly until the potatoes look "dry." Remove to a serving dish, sprinkle the lemon juice and cilantro on top, and serve hot.

EACH SERVING PROVIDES
73 calories, 1.7 g protein, 16.4 g carbohydrate
0.3 g fat, 6 mg sodium, 0 mg cholesterol

SERVING SUGGESTION

This dish complements tofu with green and red peppers (page 200) with warm spinach flat bread (page 210) and tomato, cucumber, and onion relish (page 247). It's also great for stuffing pita pockets or green bell peppers.

SAVORY STUFFED POTATOES

YIELD: 3 SERVINGS

In this dish, yogurt adds the creamy consistency in the stuffing. You can microwave the potatoes to cut down on the baking time. One large potato, pierced with a fork, microwaves in 4 to 5 minutes. Do not overcook the potatoes, or they will fall apart when stuffing.

3 large potatoes, baked
¼ cup sliced onion, rinsed and drained
1 clove garlic
Salt and pepper to taste
1 tablespoon chopped cilantro or parsley
¾ cup nonfat plain yogurt
Pinch of paprika

Preheat the oven to 450 degrees F. Cut the potatoes lengthwise through the middle and carefully scoop out the centers of the two halves with a spoon. Reserve the shells. In a food processor, mix the onion, garlic, salt, pepper, cilantro, and scooped-out potato and process. Add the yogurt gradually and process to a soft, smooth puree. Adjust seasonings and herbs. Fill the potato shells with this mixture, sprinkle the paprika on top, and bake for 15 minutes. Serve.

EACH SERVING PROVIDES
259 calories, 8.1 g protein, 56.8 g carbohydrate
0.3 g fat, 61 mg sodium, 1 mg cholesterol

SERVING SUGGESTION

Serve with Moroccan couscous with vegetables (page 136) and Greek bean and artichoke salad (page 52).

ROASTED PUFFED RICE SNACK

YIELD: 2 SERVINGS

The least expensive ingredient in the cereal section of your supermarket also makes the tastiest snack. Puffed rice dry-roasted to a crisp is light, savory, and nutritious, and it's a good alternative to potato chips or buttered popcorn. This hot and spicy snack is a meal in itself, or it can be eaten between meals; however, it must be served immediately after it is put together so that the puffed rice remains somewhat crispy. The chopped onion in this recipe should be rinsed, drained, and allowed to dry before mixing so that the puffed rice does not get soggy.

1 cup puffed rice
1 cup boiled, peeled, and diced potato
1 cup peeled and diced cucumber
⅓ cup finely chopped onion, rinsed, drained, and allowed to dry
2 tablespoons lemon juice
2 fresh hot green chili peppers, finely chopped
Salt to taste
Cayenne to taste

Place a 3-quart stainless steel saucepan on medium-high heat, add the rice puffs, and stir constantly for 1½ minutes, until they turn an almond color. Remove puffs from heat and transfer into a bowl. Add potato, cucumber, onion, lemon juice, chili peppers, salt, and cayenne. Adjust seasoning and lemon juice to taste. Serve immediately.

EACH SERVING PROVIDES
134 calories, 3.5 g protein, 31.6 g carbohydrate
0.3 g fat, 7 mg sodium, 0 mg cholesterol

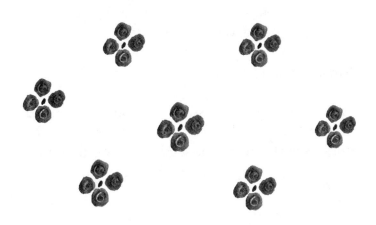

RATATOUILLE

YIELD: 6 SERVINGS

Perfect seasoning and the right blend of spices give the taste of the French Provençal region to this zesty dish. Combine any of your favorite vegetables.

½ teaspoon dried basil
½ teaspoon dried thyme
4 heaping tablespoons processed onion
2 teaspoons processed garlic
8 fresh medium tomatoes, chopped
8 cups vegetables cut into 1-inch pieces
    (any combination of eggplant, carrots, green
    bell peppers, and red bell peppers)
2 tablespoons red wine vinegar
Salt and pepper to taste

Heat an 8-quart stainless steel pot on medium-high heat. Add the basil and thyme and cook for 30 seconds. Add the onion and garlic and cook for 3 minutes. Add the tomatoes, vegetables, vinegar, salt, and pepper. Reduce the heat to low, cover, and cook for 25 minutes or until vegetables are just tender, not mushy. Serve hot.

EACH SERVING PROVIDES
99 calories, 3.4 g protein, 22.7 g carbohydrate
0.9 g fat, 51 mg sodium, 0 mg cholesterol

SERVING SUGGESTION

Garlic toast (page 214) and vegetarian scramble (page 204) with hot jalapeño dip (page 238) go well with this dish.

STUFFED SHELLS

YIELD: 8 SERVINGS

Vegetables mixed with fat-free ricotta makes eating healthier. In this fat-free version of a traditional Italian entree, vegetables add color and nutrition. Chopped, cooked, and drained spinach is a good substitute for peas and carrots.

Shells
3 cups frozen peas and carrots
1 cup fat-free ricotta cheese
16 large shells
Salt and pepper to taste

Sauce
2 cups tomato sauce
1 teaspoon processed garlic
1 heaping tablespoon processed onion
½ teaspoon oregano
½ teaspoon basil
1 tablespoon red wine vinegar
½ cup finely diced green bell pepper
Salt and pepper to taste

In a covered microwave-safe dish, microwave the peas and carrots on high for 6 minutes or put the vegetables and ¼ cup water in a saucepan, cover, and cook on low heat for 20 minutes or until tender. Drain any juices from the vegetables and set vegetables aside.

Cook the shells according to package directions, rinse in cold water, drain, and set aside. Mix peas and carrots with the ricotta and add salt and pepper. Fill each shell with the ricotta-vegetable mixture.

To make the sauce, mix the tomato sauce, garlic, onion, oregano, basil, vinegar, green pepper, salt, and pepper in a microwave-safe bowl, cover, and microwave on high for 2 minutes. Alternatively, mix all sauce ingredients, except the green peppers, in a saucepan and bring to a boil over high heat. Turn heat to low, cover pot, and simmer, about 8 minutes. Add the green peppers, cover pan again, and cook on medium heat for 3 minutes.

In a baking dish, spread a thin layer of sauce and lay the stuffed shells in rows in the dish. Pour the remaining sauce over the shells. If cooking in the microwave, cover dish and microwave for 4 to 5 minutes or until heated through. If cooking in the oven, cover shells with foil and bake in a preheated 350 degree F oven for 25 minutes. Serve hot.

EACH SERVING PROVIDES
286 calories, 14.5 g protein, 55.5 g carbohydrate
1.3 g fat, 477 mg sodium, 5 mg cholesterol

SERVING SUGGESTION
Serve with fat-free breadsticks and a green salad.

SPICY MIXED VEGETABLES

YIELD: 4 SERVINGS

Almost any frozen mixed vegetables cook well this way. If you do not have a microwave, add the frozen vegetables and salt to the spice and onion mixture and cook in a covered pan over low heat for 25 minutes.

1 (20-ounce) package frozen mixed vegetable
  (any kind)
½ teaspoon black mustard or cumin seeds
1 teaspoon ground cumin
½ teaspoon turmeric
1 cup sliced onion, rinsed and drained
Salt to taste
1 tablespoon lemon juice

Cover and microwave the vegetables on high, about 7 minutes or until vegetables are crisp-tender. Drain the vegetables and set aside.

Place a 6-quart stainless steel saucepan on medium-high heat. Add the mustard seeds and stir for 1 minute. As soon as the seeds begin to pop, lower the heat. Add the ground cumin and turmeric and stir for 1 minute. Add the onion and cook for 2 minutes. Add the vegetables and salt and stir, 3 minutes. Add the lemon juice and serve hot.

EACH SERVING PROVIDES
68 calories, 3.8 g protein, 13.6 g carbohydrate
0.3 g fat, 38 mg sodium, 0 mg cholesterol

SERVING SUGGESTION

For a meatless, protein-enriched meal, serve this dish with savory chickpeas (page 134), elegant rice with mushrooms (page 220), and cucumber yogurt relish (page 248). This dish also complements classic chicken curry (page 96) or tomato fish with black mustard seeds (page 76), green salad, lime pickle (page 244), and wild rice.

SPINACH-POTATO TOSS-UP

YIELD: 3 SERVINGS

Here's an innovative recipe when you need some inspiration. Extra-firm lowfat tofu cut into cubes may replace the potatoes (the tofu requires very little cooking time and may be added with the spinach).

1 (10-ounce) package frozen chopped spinach, thawed but not drained
4 sprigs fresh dill
3 scallions, finely sliced (green ends included)
1 teaspoon processed garlic
1 teaspoon processed or peeled and finely grated fresh ginger
1 cup peeled and diced (1-inch pieces) potatoes
2 tablespoons canned crushed tomatoes or tomato puree
2 tablespoons nonfat plain yogurt
Salt to taste

Puree the spinach and dill in a food processor for a few seconds. Place a 4-quart stainless steel saucepan on medium-high heat. Add the scallions, garlic, and ginger and stir well, about 2 minutes. Mix in the potatoes and tomatoes, lower heat, cover, and cook for 10 minutes. Add the spinach mixture, yogurt, and salt and continue stirring, about 3 minutes. Cover and simmer for 6 minutes. Serve hot.

EACH SERVING PROVIDES
91 calories, 5.1 g protein, 19.3 g carbohydrate
0.3 g fat, 133 mg sodium, 0 mg cholesterol

SERVING SUGGESTION

Gourmet black-eyed peas (page 124), tabbouleh (page 60), and white rice go well with this dish.

TOFU WITH GREEN AND RED PEPPERS

YIELD: 3 SERVINGS

Scientific research indicates that tofu not only lowers cholesterol but also prevents certain cancers because of a substance called protease inhibitors found in soybeans. Consequently, we've made every effort to introduce as many interesting recipes as possible with this remarkable food. Scallions, bell peppers, and spices add flavor to the tofu.

½ teaspoon black mustard seeds
½ teaspoon dried thyme
1 teaspoon turmeric
3 large scallions, finely sliced
½ teaspoon processed garlic
½ teaspoon processed ginger
1 cup sliced red bell pepper (1-inch pieces)
1 cup sliced green bell pepper (1-inch pieces)
½ pound extra-firm lowfat tofu, drained and cut
   into 1-inch squares
Salt to taste
2 tablespoons lemon juice or to taste

Place a 6-quart stainless steel saucepan on medium-high heat. Add the mustard seeds and stir for 40 seconds or until they begin to pop. Reduce heat to low, add the thyme and turmeric, and cook for another few seconds. Add the scallions, garlic, ginger, red and green peppers, tofu, and salt, cover, and cook for 4 minutes or until peppers are crisp-tender. Remove the cover, raise the heat to high, and cook briskly for 1 minute. Stir in lemon juice and serve hot.

EACH SERVING PROVIDES
64 calories, 6.5 g protein, 8.5 g carbohydrate
1.2 g fat, 83 mg sodium, 0 mg cholesterol

SERVING SUGGESTION

Serve over rice, roll into a warmed tortilla, or stuff in a pita pocket and top with hot chutney for a savory meal.

VEGETABLE FRITTERS

YIELD: 12 VEGETABLE FRITTERS

This dish was inspired by the Southern favorite, fried green tomatoes. In this version, slices of eggplant and zucchini squash are coated with a spicy herb batter and browned on a nonstick pan; the batter provides a coating to seal in the vegetable juices. This recipe can easily be doubled or tripled (⅓ teaspoon ground cumin should be added each time the recipe is doubled). The size of the vegetable slices may vary. Leftovers can be reheated in the microwave or in a warm oven.

3 heaping tablespoons cornmeal flour
3 heaping tablespoons all-purpose flour
½ teaspoon ground cumin
½ teaspoon dried thyme
1 teaspoon baking powder
2 tablespoons chopped fresh parsley
¼ cup lemon juice
Salt to taste
¼ cup water
Nonstick cooking spray
6 slices each eggplant and zucchini (about
    3 inches in diameter and ¼ inch thick)

In a bowl, mix the flours, cumin, thyme, baking powder, parsley, lemon juice, and salt. Gradually stir in the water (more or less water may be needed) to form a thick batter.

Set a large nonstick frying pan on medium-high heat. When hot, spray lightly with nonstick cooking spray. With a pair of tongs, dip the vegetable slices in the batter, making sure they are well coated. (If the batter gets too thin, stir in 1 teaspoon each of cornmeal flour and all-purpose flour and adjust seasoning.) Immediately place the batter-coated vegetables in the hot pan (extra batter can be spooned on top of the vegetable slices in the pan). Brown on both sides. Make sure the vegetables are cooked by piercing a knife through the center of the slices. If the vegetables are not completely cooked, lower the heat, cover, and cook until just tender. Serve hot.

EACH SERVING PROVIDES
32 calories, 1.1 g protein, 6.6 g carbohydrate
0.4 g fat, 29 mg sodium, 0 mg cholesterol

SERVING SUGGESTION

Serve as a vegetarian appetizer with tangy green cilantro chutney (page 232) or hot sauce.

VEGETARIAN SCRAMBLE

YIELD: 4 SERVINGS

Scallions lend flavor to tofu in this quick breakfast or lunch entree. Leftovers keep well in the refrigerator for 2 or 3 days. For quick substitutions, you can easily use canned tomatoes instead of the fresh ones and cilantro in place of the dill.

1 pound extra-firm lowfat tofu
Nonstick cooking spray
1 cup finely sliced scallions (green ends included)
1 cup finely diced fresh tomato
½ cup chopped fresh dill or fresh parsley
Salt and pepper to taste
Sprigs of fresh dill

Drain water from the block of tofu. With the back of a fork, crumble the tofu and set aside. Place a 12-inch nonstick frying pan on medium-high heat. When hot, spray evenly with nonstick cooking spray, add the scallions, and sauté for 2 minutes. Add the tomato and sauté for 1 minute. Add the tofu, dill, salt, and pepper, raise heat to high, and stir briskly for 2 minutes. Garnish with fresh dill. Serve hot.

EACH SERVING PROVIDES
64 calories, 8.8 g protein, 4.9 g carbohydrate
1.6 g fat, 114 mg sodium, 0 mg cholesterol

SERVING SUGGESTION

Serve on toasted English muffin or whole wheat toast.

SKEWERED VEGETABLES

YIELD: 3 SERVINGS

This is a quick stove-top version of grilled vegetables. This recipe can very easily be doubled or tripled. Cherry tomatoes, carrots, and peppers also taste great with this marinade.

1 large zucchini
12 medium fresh white mushrooms
8 small whole onions, peeled
$\frac{1}{3}$ cup Oriental dip (page 240)
6 bamboo skewers, dipped in water and drained

Cut the zucchini into 4 sections. Slice each section lengthwise into thirds. Wash and drain the mushrooms. In a bowl, marinate the vegetables in the dip. Alternate the vegetables on the skewers. Set a 12-inch nonstick frying pan on medium heat. Place the skewered vegetables in the pan and drizzle the marinade over them. Cover, turn the heat to low, and cook for 8 minutes or until the vegetables are just cooked, turning the skewers once during cooking. Serve hot.

EACH SERVING PROVIDES
86 calories, 5.1 g protein, 17.5 g carbohydrate
0.7 g fat, 651 mg sodium, 0 mg cholesterol

SERVING SUGGESTION

Serve over steamed spicy couscous or plain white rice.

WILTED KOREAN SPINACH

YIELD: 2 SERVINGS

Wilted spinach can be served as a side dish or as a bed for fish. Rice vinegar (available in supermarkets and Asian markets) provides the mellow taste.

8 cups (or 10-ounce bag) fresh chopped spinach
1 teaspoon white rice vinegar
1 teaspoon fresh lime juice
1 teaspoon low-sodium soy sauce

In a 5-quart stainless steel saucepan, add all the ingredients. Cover and cook on low heat until the spinach is just wilted, about 4 minutes. Remove the cover, raise the heat to high, and cook briskly for a minute to reduce the spinach juice. Serve hot.

EACH SERVING PROVIDES
50 calories, 6.6 g protein, 8.3 g carbohydrate
0.8 g fat, 101 mg sodium, 0 mg cholesterol

SERVING SUGGESTION
Serve as a bed for a fillet of fish with spicy stuffing (page 78) with rice and Athenian eggplant with herbs (page 142).

BREADS AND
RICE DISHES

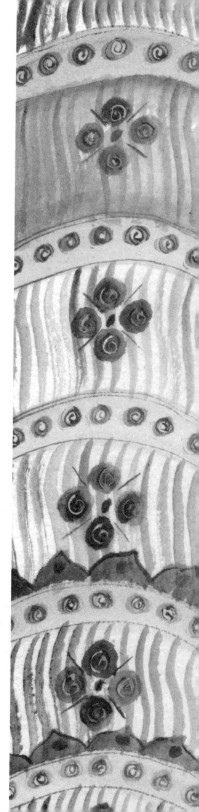

SPINACH FLAT BREAD

YIELD: 10 FLAT BREADS

The dough for this flat bread is made with a combination of whole wheat flour and frozen chopped spinach (the moisture in the spinach replaces fat for a soft texture). Spinach flat bread can be refrigerated for a week and frozen for months. It heats well in the microwave (for each flat bread, about 20 seconds on high in a covered dish) or in a skillet on the stove.

2 cups whole wheat flour
1 (10-ounce) package chopped frozen spinach, thawed but not drained
¼ cup water

In a food processor, add the flour, spinach, and water. Process the mixture to start forming a dough. If necessary, add more water, 1 tablespoon at a time, to make the dough the consistency of pizza dough. If the dough is too sticky, add more flour and continue processing. Remove the dough from the food processor and knead by hand to make it pliable. At this point, the dough may be refrigerated or frozen for use at a later time.

Divide the dough into ten equal-size small balls, slightly smaller than golf balls. Dust each ball with whole wheat flour and roll out into 6- to 7-inch disks. Sprinkle whole wheat flour while rolling, if necessary, to prevent sticking.

Heat a skillet over medium-high heat, making sure it gets fairly hot (to prevent the dough from sticking). Have a pair of tongs handy to flip the flat bread over. Turn on another burner to medium-high heat and put a cake rack over it. Place the rolled dough on the hot skillet and cook, about 10 seconds, then flip to the other side with the tongs and cook for another 10 seconds. Small brown-black spots will appear on both sides. Lift the half cooked bread with the tongs and place it directly on the cake rack over the flame and cook, about 30 seconds on each side. Do not let it blacken, burn, or smoke (the process is a very quick one).

Place the cooked bread in a container lined with a paper towel and with a snug lid (such as a Corning dish). After all the flat bread is stacked, place another paper towel on top of them and cover tightly. The paper towel will absorb the moisture caused by the steam. Serve hot.

EACH SERVING PROVIDES
90 calories, 4.2 g protein, 18.9 g carbohydrate
0.5 g fat, 26 mg sodium, 0 mg cholesterol

SERVING SUGGESTION

Roll vegetable leftovers, spicy mixed vegetables (page 196), or ground turkey with peas (page 104) in the bread, along with slices of homemade pickled onion (page 242), and secure with a toothpick for a neat lunch. This can be heated in a microwave for about 40 seconds per roll. Serve with pickles or hot chutney on the side.

Breads and Rice Dishes

ASPARAGUS-MUSHROOM CROSTINI

YIELD: 6 CROSTINI

Crostini are "little crusts" of toasted bread generally served at the beginning of an Italian meal. These toasted slices of crusty French or Italian bread, with a variety of toppings, may also accompany an entree.

8 ounces sliced fresh white mushrooms
1 (14-ounce) can green asparagus
   (spears and tips included)
Nonstick cooking spray
1 cup finely diced onion
1 teaspoon processed garlic
5 fresh large basil leaves, or ½ teaspoon dried basil
½ cup finely chopped parsley
Salt and pepper to taste
½ loaf French bread
Fresh parsley sprigs

Preheat the oven or toaster oven to 350 degrees F. Rinse the mushrooms and drain. Place the mushrooms in a food processor and press the Pulse button 4 to 5 times until mushrooms are diced. Do not overprocess. Drain the asparagus and cut into ¼-inch pieces.

Set a 12-inch nonstick frying pan or a 5-quart nonstick pot on medium heat, spray lightly with nonstick cooking spray, add the onion and garlic, and sauté for 2 minutes. Add the chopped mushrooms, asparagus, basil, parsley, salt, and pepper and cook for another 2 minutes. Increase heat to high to enable vegetable juices to evaporate. The mixture should look "dry." Turn off heat and set aside.

Slice the French bread at a diagonal angle into ½-inch-thick slices. Toast the slices until they are golden brown. Top each slice with the asparagus-mushroom mixture. Garnish with parsley and serve warm.

EACH SERVING PROVIDES
148 calories, 6.3 g protein, 26.9 g carbohydrate
1.5 g fat, 231 mg sodium, 0 mg cholesterol

SERVING SUGGESTION

The crostini are excellent alongside chicken cacciatore (page 88) or tri-pepper pasta (page 170) and a tossed salad.

GARLIC TOAST

YIELD: 4 GARLIC TOASTS

This recipe can be doubled or tripled with ease. The processed garlic should be added very sparingly (⅓ teaspoon of garlic powder can be used instead of fresh garlic). Using canned peeled tomatoes will save you some time; be sure to squeeze as much juice as possible from the tomatoes before chopping to ensure that the toast does not become soggy.

6 canned whole, peeled tomatoes
¼ teaspoon processed garlic
2 tablespoons finely chopped parsley
¼ teaspoon dried oregano
Salt and pepper to taste
2 (2½-inch-thick) slices French bread
    (diagonally cut)
Fat-free parmesan cheese to taste

Squeeze as much juice as possible from the tomatoes and finely chop. In a bowl, mix the tomatoes with garlic, parsley, oregano, salt, and pepper. With a sharp knife, cut each bread slice in half, to make

4 diagonal halves in all. Toast the slices until golden brown. Spread about 2 teaspoons of the tomato-garlic mixture on each slice. Sprinkle with cheese and serve immediately.

EACH SERVING PROVIDES
120 calories, 4.0 g protein, 22.4 g carbohydrate
1.3 g fat, 360 mg sodium, 0 mg cholesterol

SERVING SUGGESTION
••
Serve with chicken cacciatore (page 88) and a green salad.

FRAGRANT BASMATI RICE

YIELD: 3 SERVINGS

Basmati, a popular fragrant rice, is grown in the foothills of the Himalayas in northern India. This slender long-grain rice absorbs spices easily, cooks quickly, and is an ideal accompaniment to most cuisines. Cooked basmati rice, without oil, will not stick like other types of rice and is therefore ideal for fat-free cooking (all rice preparations in this book call for basmati rice). The grains break apart very easily and must be handled gently.

Basmati rice requires $1\frac{1}{2}$ times the measure of water to 1 measure of rice. The measurement has to be precise, because excess water will result in overcooked and sticky rice.

1 cup basmati rice
$1\frac{1}{2}$ cups water

Rinse the rice by putting it in a bowl and filling it with water till the rice is submerged about 1 inch deep. Carefully move the water around and pour away the milky water. Repeat the process. In a 3-quart stainless steel saucepan, combine the rice and the water and bring to a boil on medium-high heat. Reduce the heat to low, cover the pot, and cook for about 15 minutes or until the water has been absorbed. Turn off the heat and fluff the rice gently with a fork. Replace the cover until you are ready to serve, to retain heat and moisture.

EACH SERVING PROVIDES

223 calories, 4.3 g protein, 48.8 g carbohydrate

0.4 g fat, 6 mg sodium, 0 mg cholesterol

SERVING SUGGESTION

Basmati rice is ideal with classic chicken curry (page 96) or spicy "stir-fried" potatoes (page 186) and savory chickpeas (page 134).

VERMICELLI RICE, MEXICAN-STYLE

YIELD: 4 SERVINGS

In this dish, angel hair pasta or vermicelli, broken up into bits, work very well. Dry-roasting the pasta pieces before adding it to the other ingredients eliminates the need for oil to sauté the pasta. The hot sauce and chili powder provide just the right amount of spice.

1 cup basmati rice
½ cup vermicelli broken into ½-inch pieces
3 heaping tablespoons processed onion
2 teaspoons processed garlic
1 teaspoon chili powder
4 canned whole tomatoes, drained and chopped
1 cup frozen peas
1 cup frozen cut corn
1 cup diced green bell pepper
2 tablespoons hot sauce
1½ cups water
Salt to taste

Rinse the rice gently, drain, and set aside.

Place a 4-quart stainless steel saucepan on medium-high heat. Add the vermicelli pieces and stir for 1½ minutes or until they turn light brown. Put the roasted pasta in a small bowl and set aside. Replace the saucepan on medium-high heat, add the onion, garlic, and chili powder, and stir, about 3 minutes, taking care the mixture does not burn. Add the tomatoes, peas, corn, green pepper, rice, roasted vermicelli bits, hot sauce, water, and salt, cover, and cook on low heat until water is absorbed and rice and vermicelli are cooked. Keep covered until ready to serve.

EACH SERVING PROVIDES
331 calories, 10.0 g protein, 71.1 g carbohydrate
1.3 g fat, 188 mg sodium, 0 mg cholesterol

SERVING SUGGESTION

Serve topped with gourmet black-eyed peas (page 124) and with mock guacamole (page 236) on the side.

ELEGANT RICE WITH MUSHROOMS

YIELD: 4 SERVINGS

A savory rice preparation such as this enhances any meal. This dish is especially versatile, since mushrooms are available year-round (mushroom bits and stems also work out quite well).

1½ cups basmati rice
2 tablespoons processed onion
1 teaspoon processed garlic
¼ teaspoon ground clove
¼ teaspoon ground cinnamon
1½ cups sliced fresh mushrooms or
    canned mushrooms, drained
Salt to taste
2½ cups water

Rinse the rice and carefully drain the water. Set rice aside. Place a 4-quart stainless steel saucepan on medium heat, add the onion and garlic, and cook, about 2 minutes. Add the clove and cinnamon. (This mixture may stick. Lower heat to ensure it does not burn.) Stir in the rice, mushrooms, and salt. Add the water and bring to a boil. Reduce the heat to low, cover, and cook for 12 to 15 minutes.

As soon as the water is absorbed and the rice is tender, turn off the heat and leave covered until you are ready to serve. Spoon on to a warm platter and serve immediately.

EACH SERVING PROVIDES
279 calories, 6.1 g protein, 60.9 g carbohydrate
0.7 g fat, 9 mg sodium, 0 mg cholesterol

SERVING SUGGESTION

This rice dish along with vegetarian "ground meat" with peas (page 156), spicy "stir-fried" potatoes (page 186), and a tossed salad go well together.

RICE AND GREEN PEAS

YIELD: 4 SERVINGS

A combination of rice and peas in this simple, old-time favorite converts plain rice into a fancy, quick, and delicious preparation.

2 cups basmati rice
1 cup finely sliced onion
2 bay leaves
$\frac{1}{2}$ teaspoon ground clove
$\frac{1}{2}$ teaspoon ground cumin
1 cup frozen peas
Salt to taste
$3\frac{1}{2}$ cups water

Rinse, drain, and set aside rice. Place a 4-quart stainless steel saucepan on medium heat, add the onion and bay leaves, and cook for 2 minutes, stirring continuously. Lower heat, add the clove, cumin, rice, peas, and salt, and stir for 1 minute. Add the water and bring to a boil on high heat. Reduce the heat to low, cover, and cook, 12 to 15 minutes or until the rice is tender. Discard the bay leaves. Remove from heat and keep covered until you are ready to serve.

EACH SERVING PROVIDES
387 calories, 9.2 g protein, 83.4 g carbohydrate
0.9 g fat, 46 mg sodium, 0 mg cholesterol

SERVING SUGGESTION

Spicy eggplant (page 144), savory stuffed potatoes (page 188), and tangy Hawaiian cabbage slaw (page 56) go well with this preparation.

ORIENTAL RICE "STIR-FRY"

YIELD: 4 SERVINGS

This is a simple rice and vegetable combination and a great way to use up leftover rice. Tofu provides the protein in this colorful vegetarian medley. You can adjust the soy sauce and omit the salt if you wish.

3 tablespoons low-sodium soy sauce
3 tablespoons white rice vinegar
$\frac{1}{3}$ pound extra-firm lowfat tofu, sliced into squares 1 inch by 1 inch by $\frac{1}{8}$ inch thick
3 scallions, finely sliced (green ends included)
1 teaspoon processed garlic
2 cups frozen peas and carrots
Salt to taste
2 cups cooked white rice
1 cup bean sprouts

Combine the soy sauce, vinegar, and tofu in a bowl and set aside. Heat a 5-quart nonstick stainless steel pot on medium heat, add the scallions and garlic, and sauté for 2 minutes. Reduce the heat to low, add the peas and carrots, and season with salt.

Cover and cook for 5 minutes or until vegetables are cooked. Add the tofu along with the marinade, rice, and bean sprouts. Raise the heat to high and stir well until the rice is heated through. Serve hot.

EACH SERVING PROVIDES
206 calories, 9.7 g protein, 40.6 g carbohydrate
1.2 g fat, 551 mg sodium, 0 mg cholesterol

SERVING SUGGESTION
••
Brazilian black bean soup (page 34) for starters, this dish, and a fruit salad make a balanced meal.

RICE-VEGETABLE PILAF

YIELD: 6 SERVINGS

This festive vegetable and rice dish can be served with almost any cuisine, and it can be started ahead of time; the final step (adding the water and cooking) can be done just before serving. Almost any kind of frozen vegetables can be used.

2 cups basmati rice
1 teaspoon cumin seeds
1 teaspoon ground cumin
½ teaspoon ground coriander
1 teaspoon turmeric
1 teaspoon processed garlic
2 cups frozen vegetables (peas, carrots, corn, or any combination)
Salt to taste
3½ cups water

Rinse the rice, carefully drain the water, and set rice aside. Place a 4-quart stainless steel saucepan on medium-high heat, add the cumin seeds, and cook for 1 minute or until the seeds begin to pop. Lower the heat, add the ground cumin, coriander, and turmeric and stir for 1 minute. Add the garlic, increase the heat to medium-high, and stir for another minute. Mix in the vegetables, rice, and salt. Add the water and bring to a boil. Lower the heat and cover with a snug-fitting lid. Cook for 12 to 15 minutes or until the water is absorbed and the rice and vegetables are cooked. Remove from heat and leave covered until ready to serve.

EACH SERVING PROVIDES

270 calories, 7.3 g protein, 57.1 g carbohydrate

0.8 g fat, 55 mg sodium, 0 mg cholesterol

SERVING SUGGESTION

For a delicious, protein-rich meal, serve with gourmet black-eyed peas (page 124) and a mixed green salad.

SAVORY YELLOW RICE

YIELD: 4 SERVINGS

The contrast of black mustard seeds and yellow turmeric gives this dish its rich color and flavor.

1 cup basmati rice
2 bay leaves
½ teaspoon black mustard seeds
½ teaspoon turmeric
Salt to taste
1½ cups water

Rinse the rice, carefully drain the water, and set rice aside. Heat a 3-quart stainless steel pot on medium-high heat, add the bay leaves and mustard seeds, and stir for 1 minute or until the seeds begin to pop. Immediately reduce the heat to low, add the turmeric, and stir for a few seconds (the turmeric will smoke due to the absence of oil). Stir in the rice, salt, and water and increase the heat to medium-high. Bring the rice a boil. Cover, reduce the heat to low, and cook, about 12 minutes or until all the water is absorbed and the rice is tender. Discard the bay leaves and fluff the rice gently with a fork. Leave covered until you are ready to serve. Just before serving, spoon onto a serving platter.

EACH SERVING PROVIDES
171 calories, 3.4 g protein, 37.2 g carbohydrate
0.4 g fat, 11 mg sodium, 0 mg cholesterol

SERVING SUGGESTION
••
Serve with button mushrooms in tomato sauce (page 160) or classic chicken curry (page 96) and cucumber yogurt relish (page 248).

CHUTNEYS, DIPS, PICKLES, RELISHES, AND YOGURT

TANGY GREEN CILANTRO CHUTNEY

YIELD: 2 CUPS

Green chutney can be made hot or mild to taste, depending on the number and the kind of chili pepper that is added. This zippy chutney goes well on a chicken patty, tuna patty, veggie burger, or bagel. It can be made in large quantities and frozen, and it will last up to one week in the refrigerator. The recipe for chutney fish (page 66) requires this preparation.

3 hot green chili peppers or jalapeño peppers
Juice of 1 lemon
1 cup chopped tomatoes, fresh or canned
Salt to taste
1 large onion, peeled, chopped, rinsed,
    and drained
2 cups fresh cilantro leaves and small stems
1 clove garlic

Put all the ingredients in a food processor and process for a few seconds until pureed. Adjust the lemon juice, chili pepper, and salt according to taste. Serve immediately or store in an airtight container and refrigerate or freeze.

EACH TABLESPOON PROVIDES
8 calories, 0.3 g protein, 1.7 g carbohydrate
0.1 g fat, 3 mg sodium, 0 mg cholesterol

SERVING SUGGESTION

Serve with chicken, tuna, or vegetable patties, as a spicy spread on a toasted bagel, or as an accompaniment with any meal as a relish.

TANGY TOMATO-GINGER CHUTNEY

YIELD: 1 CUP

The fresh, gingery taste of tomato chutney goes well with both spicy and simple food. This tangy accompaniment for most meals can be made hot or mild, depending on the number of hot peppers that are added. Chili peppers may be seeded to reduce their "bite." The chutney will last up to one week in the refrigerator or can be frozen to last longer.

½ teaspoon black mustard seeds
1 teaspoon freshly grated or processed ginger
1 hot green chili pepper or jalapeño pepper, diced
1 tablespoon brown sugar
1 cup canned tomatoes (about 6 tomatoes), chopped
2 tablespoons distilled white vinegar
Salt to taste

Set a 3-quart stainless steel saucepan on medium-high heat. Add the mustard seeds and wait until they begin to pop. Immediately add the ginger, chili pepper, sugar, tomatoes, vinegar, and salt and bring to a boil. Cover and cook on low heat for about 6 minutes. Serve hot or at room temperature.

EACH TABLESPOON PROVIDES
8 calories, 0.2 g protein, 1.9 g carbohydrate
0.1 g fat, 26 mg sodium, 0 mg cholesterol

Chutneys, Dips, Pickles, Relishes, and Yogurt
....

CREAMY CELERY AND ONION DIP

YIELD: 1 CUP

Yogurt cheese gives this dip a rich, creamy consistency; the hot sauce and cilantro add pungent flavor. Fresh chopped dill may replace the cilantro for an interesting variation. Be sure to rinse the onions before adding to reduce the strong flavor. The dip will last for two to three days in the refrigerator.

1 cup yogurt cheese (page 252)
2 tablespoons finely diced celery
2 tablespoons finely diced onion, rinsed and drained
2 tablespoons finely chopped cilantro leaves
3 teaspoons hot sauce, or to taste
¼ teaspoon salt, or to taste

In a bowl, mix all ingredients. Adjust seasoning according to taste. Cover and chill. Mix well before serving.

EACH TABLESPOON PROVIDES
15 calories, 0.8 g protein, 1.7 g carbohydrate
0.1 g fat, 44 mg sodium, 1 mg cholesterol

SERVING SUGGESTION

Serve with a platter of crisp vegetables, such as cauliflower florets, broccoli, carrot sticks, and peppers.

Chutneys, Dips, Pickles, Relishes, and Yogurt

MOCK GUACAMOLE

Canned green beans, asparagus, and frozen peas are used in place of avocados in this Mexican dip. It can be stored for three days in the refrigerator.

1 (8-ounce) can cut green asparagus, drained
⅓ cup canned cut green beans, drained
½ cup frozen peas, thawed, cooked, and drained
1 clove garlic
3 tablespoons lime juice
1 small tomato, finely chopped
1 tablespoon finely chopped onion,
    rinsed and drained
Salt to taste
Sprig of cilantro

Process the asparagus, green beans, cooked peas, and garlic in a food processor to form a smooth puree. In a bowl, mix the puree with the lime juice, tomato, onion, and salt. Garnish with a cilantro sprig. Cover and chill until ready to use.

EACH TABLESPOON PROVIDES
11 calories, 0.7 g protein, 2.1 g carbohydrate
0.1 g fat, 13 mg sodium, 0 mg cholesterol

SERVING SUGGESTION

Serve with Mexican-style bean burritos (page 120) or vegetarian fajitas (page 148), or use as a sandwich spread.

JALAPEÑO DIP

YIELD: 2 CUPS

Salsa, as this dip is popularly called, can be made hot or mild. Jalapeño peppers can be seeded to reduce their bite; half a green bell pepper in place of the jalapeño peppers will make the dip very mild. It works as a chutney, relish, sandwich spread, or dip for cocktail patties. This dip keeps for one week in the refrigerator and freezes well.

6 jalapeño peppers, washed and sliced
2 medium onions, chopped
8 canned whole tomatoes, drained
¼ cup distilled white vinegar
2 tablespoons tomato paste
Salt to taste

Put all ingredients in a food processor and process for a few seconds until the ingredients are chopped into small bits. Do not overprocess. Serve at room temperature or store in an airtight container in the refrigerator or freezer.

EACH TABLESPOON PROVIDES
11 calories, 0.4 g protein, 2.5 g carbohydrate
0.1 g fat, 28 mg sodium, 0 mg cholesterol

SERVING SUGGESTION

Use as a sandwich spread or dip, or serve as a relish alongside any meal or as a topping for tuna kebabs (page 80) or vegetable patties (page 174).

Chutneys, Dips, Pickles, Relishes, and Yogurt

ORIENTAL DIP

YIELD: 2/3 CUP

Oriental dip is an ideal marinade for grilling skewered vegetables (fresh vegetables may also be "stir-fried" on a nonstick frying pan on medium-high heat). The mellow flavor of rice vinegar blends well with the vegetables. The recipe for skewered vegetables (page 206) requires this preparation. The dip will last for one week in the refrigerator.

3 tablespoons low-sodium soy sauce
3 tablespoons lemon juice
1 teaspoon processed garlic
3 tablespoons white rice vinegar
Salt and pepper to taste

Mix all ingredients in a glass bowl. Cover and keep refrigerated.

EACH TABLESPOON PROVIDES
5 calories, 0.4 g protein, 1.2 g carbohydrate
0 g fat, 213 mg sodium, 0 mg cholesterol

SERVING SUGGESTION

Use as a marinade for cooking fresh vegetables, such as sliced zucchini; whole mushrooms; whole, peeled, broiler onions; and chunks of bell peppers.

CREAMY SPINACH DIP

YIELD: ⅔ CUP

Yogurt cheese is the base for this delicious lowfat dip. It can be served immediately or refrigerated for two days. Spinach emits its juice during refrigeration, so be sure to stir well before serving.

2 tablespoons chopped frozen spinach, thawed
½ cup yogurt cheese (page 252)
2 tablespoons lemon juice
1 teaspoon processed onion
½ teaspoon processed garlic
Salt and pepper to taste

Squeeze the juice from the spinach. In a bowl, mix the spinach into the yogurt cheese. Add the lemon juice, onion, garlic, salt, and pepper. Adjust seasoning to taste. Serve immediately or cover and chill. Stir well just before serving.

EACH TABLESPOON PROVIDES
13 calories, 0.7 g protein, 1.9 g carbohydrate
0 g fat, 5 mg sodium, 0 mg cholesterol

SERVING SUGGESTION

Serve as a dip with fresh vegetable sticks or as a topping for baked potatoes.

HOMEMADE PICKLED ONIONS

YIELD: 8 CUPS

Pickled onions perk up a simple meal. They are an appetizing sandwich filler and can be chopped and added to a dip. The natural, rich red color of the beets "bleed" onto the carrots and onions. This pickle will keep for months in the refrigerator. In time, the onions will soften and mellow in flavor. Do not discard the leftover vinegar when the pickled vegetables are finished; this flavored vinegar can be used to spice up soups, stews, salad dressings, and marinades.

4 medium carrots, peeled, washed, and sliced into thin 1-inch-long sticks
2 large onions, peeled, sliced, rinsed, and drained
1 (15-ounce) can sliced beets, drained and halved
3 tablespoons salt
4 cups red wine vinegar

In a large bowl, mix the carrots, onions, and beets. Transfer the vegetables to a ½-gallon (64-ounce) clear plastic or glass jar with a lid. Add the salt. Pour enough vinegar to just cover the vegetables. Close the jar tightly and shake well to mix. Store in the refrigerator. The pickled vegetables will be ready in a week.

EACH TABLESPOON PROVIDES
5 calories, 0.1 g protein, 1.4 g carbohydrate
0 g fat, 164 mg sodium, 0 mg cholesterol

SERVING SUGGESTION

With a clean, dry spoon, transfer as much as needed to a small bowl and serve with meals as a relish.

LIME PICKLE

YIELD: 2 CUPS

Lime pickle is made during the hot summer season. Limes, cut in small pieces, are marinated in spices and kept out in the hot sun every day for about two weeks. This softens the fruit and gives it a delicious, tangy flavor. The salt, sugar, and black pepper act as natural preservatives and also help soften the skin of the lime. Over time, the pickle will condense to approximately half its original quantity. A clean, empty pickle jar is ideal for this use. The pickle will last indefinitely at room temperature.

6 fresh limes, washed, dried, and cut into
   ¼-inch pieces
3½ tablespoons salt
1 tablespoon ground black pepper
2 tablespoons sugar
1 teaspoon dried thyme
1 teaspoon cayenne

In a bowl, mix the limes, salt, black pepper, sugar, thyme, and cayenne. Transfer to a 32-ounce clean, dry glass jar with an airtight plastic lid, cover the opening with a piece of foil, and tighten the lid. Place the jar in the hot sun for 10 days, shaking the jar vigorously once in a while to enable the lime juice and spices to mix with the lime pieces.

The pickle is ready when the skin of the lime has softened and the pickle has turned brown. Store at room temperature. Use a clean, dry spoon when serving. Moisture of any kind, when in contact with the pickle, will cause bacteria to form and will spoil the pickle.

EACH TABLESPOON PROVIDES
7 calories, 0.1 g protein, 1.9 g carbohydrate
0.1 g fat, 699 mg sodium, 0 mg cholesterol

SERVING SUGGESTION

Serve a very small amount as a relish to perk up a meal.

DAIKON RELISH

YIELD: 4 SERVINGS

Daikon in Japanese means "large root." Now commonly available in supermarkets, this large, white vegetable is actually a radish with a fresh, crisp, and pungent flavor. Due to the overpowering aroma of grated daikon, it must be kept in a sealed container until it is ready to be served. The relish should be stored in the refrigerator and will last for two days.

2 cups peeled and coarsely grated daikon
2 tablespoons lime juice
1 tablespoon chopped fresh cilantro leaves
1 medium tomato, finely chopped
Salt to taste

Mix all ingredients, keep covered in an airtight container, and chill.

EACH SERVING PROVIDES
17 calories, 0.6 g protein, 4.0 g carbohydrate
0.2 g fat, 12 mg sodium, 0 mg cholesterol

SERVING SUGGESTION

Serve as a relish or a side salad with rice-vegetable pilaf (page 226) and tofu with green and red peppers (page 200).

TOMATO, CUCUMBER, AND ONION RELISH

YIELD: 2 SERVINGS

Relish and chutney of various kinds make meals more interesting and are a colorful addition to the table. This relish is quick and easy and these ingredients are usually on hand. It will last for one day in the refrigerator.

1 cup finely chopped onion
1 cup finely chopped tomatoes
1 cup peeled and chopped cucumber
Cayenne to taste
1 tablespoon lemon juice
Salt to taste

In a bowl, mix the onion, tomatoes, cucumber, cayenne, and lemon juice. Just before serving, add salt and mix well.

EACH SERVING PROVIDES
57 calories, 1.9 g protein, 12.5 g carbohydrate
0.5 g fat, 8 mg sodium, 0 mg cholesterol

SERVING SUGGESTION

This tasty accompaniment will liven up any meal. It may also be used for stuffing pita pockets together with spicy "stir-fried" potatoes (page 186).

CUCUMBER YOGURT RELISH

YIELD: 2 SERVINGS

Hot and spicy food is generally accompanied by this cool yogurt relish. Finely chopped fresh tomatoes or peeled and coarsely grated carrots may replace the cucumber.

½ teaspoon ground cumin
½ cucumber, peeled and coarsely grated
1 cup nonfat plain yogurt
Salt to taste
Cayenne to taste

Heat a small stainless steel saucepan on medium-high heat and roast the ground cumin for 1 minute. Set aside to cool.

In a bowl, add the cucumber, yogurt, salt, cayenne, and cumin. Mix well and adjust seasoning if necessary. Serve chilled.

EACH SERVING PROVIDES
75 calories, 7.0 g protein, 11.1 g carbohydrate
0.4 g fat, 90 mg sodium, 2 mg cholesterol

SERVING SUGGESTION
Serve with chicken biryani (page 100) and spicy potato salad (page 55).

Chutneys, Dips, Pickles, Relishes, and Yogurt
••••

NONFAT PLAIN YOGURT

YIELD: 3 CUPS

The art of yogurt making is centuries old, yet it's so simple that you can do it at home. This ancient method was devised to preserve milk in hot climates in the absence of refrigeration. Today, in many homes in the Middle and Far East, yogurt is made daily from leftover milk. Consider making a fresh, full batch each week—it is an invaluable ingredient in dips, curries, gravies, and desserts. For this recipe, use a glass bowl with a lid (Corning or Pyrex works very well).

To start the process for the first time, you will need to purchase a small container of lowfat plain yogurt containing active yogurt cultures. Later, you may use a small amount of your homemade yogurt to make fresh yogurt every time. On a warm summer day, yogurt takes only 3 to 4 hours to set. In winter, you need to insulate the yogurt container by wrapping it two or three times with a woolen shawl, or you may keep it in a warmed oven. The warm temperature helps the yogurt bacilli to multiply.

3 cups skim milk
2 tablespoons lowfat plain yogurt with active
    yogurt cultures

CONTINUED

Bring the milk to a boil in a stainless steel saucepan, stirring constantly to avoid sticking to the bottom of the pan. When the milk begins to boil and starts rising rapidly to the top of the saucepan, remove from heat to let the milk subside. Lower the heat and put the pan back on. Let the milk "roll" or simmer for about 2 minutes (this ensures that all harmful bacteria in the milk has been destroyed, which would otherwise prevent the yogurt cultures from being effective). Remove from heat, pour the milk into a clean glass bowl, and set aside to start cooling down to approximately 110 to 112 degrees F (this is the ideal temperature for the yogurt bacilli to multiply). The simple test for the right temperature is to put your clean finger into the milk. If it feels comfortably warm (like warm bath water), then the milk is ready. If your finger feels uncomfortable, let the milk cool some more, because the yogurt bacilli will not multiply at temperatures higher than 120 degrees F or below 90 degrees F.

While the milk is cooling, in a small cup, beat the yogurt with a spoon until smooth. When the milk has cooled down to a comfortably warm temperature, add 2 tablespoons of the warm milk to the yogurt and mix well. Immediately pour this milk-yogurt mixture into the glass bowl with the rest of the milk and stir well.

Cover the bowl, insulate it by wrapping a warm shawl or blanket (if the weather is cold) around it, and set the bowl aside, away from the draft. Alternatively, preheat the oven to 150 degrees F, then switch the oven off. Put the bowl in the warmed oven for 4 hours to set. Check to see if it's done. On cold days, the yogurt takes about 4 to 5 hours, or you may leave it overnight to set. To ensure that the yogurt is set, open the lid and tilt the bowl slightly. The yogurt should have the consistency of light pudding. There may be some water on the surface, which is natural in homemade yogurt. (If the yogurt is still milky and is not set at all, then the milk was not the right temperature or the yogurt that was used did not have active culture. Warm the oven to 100 degrees F, then switch the oven off. Put the bowl inside the oven to set for a couple of hours more.) Refrigerate immediately.

EACH SERVING PROVIDES

92 calories, 8.8 g protein, 12.5 g carbohydrate

0.6 g fat, 132 mg sodium, 5 mg cholesterol

SERVING SUGGESTION

The yogurt may be eaten plain, made into a relish with grated cucumber, used to make yogurt cheese, or used as a topping over fresh fruit.

YOGURT CHEESE

YIELD: $\frac{1}{2}$ CUP

Yogurt cheese—the thick creamy part of yogurt that remains once the water from the yogurt is drained—is an excellent ingredient for creamy desserts, dips, salad dressings, and as a topping for baked potatoes. Planning ahead is a good idea when yogurt cheese is required in a recipe because it takes 1 hour for the water to drain. Yogurt cheese should be made in the refrigerator, since yogurt will spoil if left out for any length of time in hot weather. A standard coffee filter accommodates 1 cup of yogurt, which will make $\frac{1}{2}$ cup of yogurt cheese. If more than 1 cup of yogurt is required, more filters will be needed. Generally, the quantity of yogurt cheese obtained is approximately half that of the yogurt.

1 cup nonfat plain yogurt

Put a coffee filter inside a mesh strainer (6 inches in diameter) and suspend the strainer over a deep glass or stainless steel bowl. Pour the yogurt into the filter and place in the refrigerator for an hour. Occasionally discard the water that collects in the bowl to ensure that it does not come in contact with the bottom of the strainer. Store the yogurt cheese in a covered container in the refrigerator and use as directed.

EACH SERVING PROVIDES
112 calories, 6.3 g protein, 12.7 g carbohydrate
0.3 g fat, 33 mg sodium, 5 mg cholesterol

DESSERTS

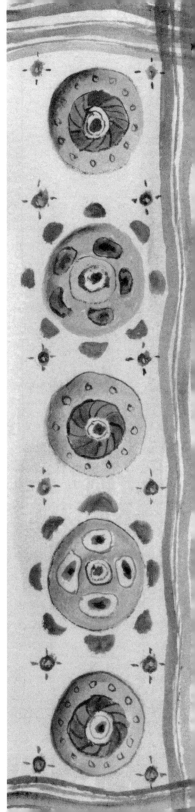

ALMOND FUDGE SQUARES

YIELD: 30 FUDGE SQUARES

This dessert can be made very quickly, but it takes quite a long time to cool because the texture is very dense. Chopped pistachios or slivered almonds are the preferred topping, but they are high in fat, so multicolored candied fruit peel is a good replacement. The fudge squares will store well for three to four days in the refrigerator, or they can be frozen for an indefinite period. To serve, thaw the required amount at room temperature.

Nonstick cooking spray
1 (2-pound) container fat-free ricotta cheese
1½ cups sugar
½ cup nonfat dry milk powder
5 tablespoons all-purpose flour
1 cup semolina
¼ teaspoon pure almond extract
1 heaping tablespoon finely sliced, candied, mixed fruit peel

Line the base and sides of an 8-inch square dish (a glass baking dish or cake pan works well) with aluminum foil, spray lightly with nonstick cooking spray, and set aside.

In a 6- or 8-quart stainless steel pot, mix the ricotta cheese, sugar, milk powder, flour, and semolina and cook on medium-high heat, stirring continuously. At first the mixture will be thin, but slowly it will start thickening. Add the almond extract. (Reduce heat, if necessary; care must be taken to ensure that the mixture does not stick to the bottom of the pan or turn brown.) Keep stirring constantly until the mixture is the consistency of soft dough; this will take about 8 minutes. Remove from heat.

Empty the mixture into the prepared dish. Using a spatula coated with nonstick cooking spray, flatten the surface of the mixture evenly. Make sure that all empty spaces and corners are filled and that the mixture takes the shape of the dish. Sprinkle the fruit peel over the mixture and press in gently with the spatula. Set aside, uncovered, to cool completely (this ensures that no moisture builds up when covered with plastic wrap). Cover with plastic wrap and refrigerate for 3 hours.

When chilled, gently lift out the fudge with the foil and place on a cutting board. Peel back the foil gently and cut into 1½-inch squares or diamond shapes (be sure to use a sharp knife for cutting). Serve chilled or at room temperature.

EACH SQUARE PROVIDES
91 calories, 5.6 g protein, 16.7 g carbohydrate
0.3 g fat, 69 mg sodium, 5 mg cholesterol

APPLE CRUMBLE

YIELD: 5 SERVINGS

Second and third helpings of this dish should not cause a twinge of guilt, as butter is replaced by the applesauce. Fresh, sweet apples are available in most supermarkets year-round. Any brand may be used, except the Granny Smith variety, which is almost always tart. Apple crumble made in large quantities requires cooking the sliced apples and applesauce on low heat, in a covered saucepan, until the apples are cooked. Cinnamon may then be added and the apples baked according to the directions below.

5 medium to large sweet apples, peeled, cored,
   halved, and thinly sliced (about 4 cups)
5 tablespoons applesauce
$\frac{1}{2}$ teaspoon ground cinnamon
$3\frac{1}{2}$ tablespoons Grape Nuts cereal
2 tablespoons dark brown sugar

Preheat the oven or toaster oven to 350 degrees F. In a bowl, mix the apples, applesauce, and cinnamon. Transfer the mixture into a $8\frac{1}{2} \times 4\frac{1}{2} \times 2\frac{1}{2}$-inch Pyrex or glass baking dish. Sprinkle evenly with the cereal. Spread the brown sugar over the cereal. Bake for about 25 minutes or until the apples are soft. Serve.

EACH SERVING PROVIDES
130 calories, 0.9 g protein, 32.7 g carbohydrate
0.6 g fat, 35 mg sodium, 0 mg cholesterol

FRUIT CREAM

YIELD: 6 SERVINGS

Yogurt cheese makes this luscious dessert easy to make. Choose ripe fresh fruit for best results. A sugar substitute will reduce the calorie content.

2 cups yogurt cheese (page 252)
4 tablespoons sugar or to taste
1 teaspoon pure vanilla extract
2 cups fresh fruit (for example, seedless whole green grapes, raspberries, sliced strawberries, mangoes, or peaches)
Few slices fresh kiwi fruit
Whole strawberries

In a dessert bowl, gently mix the yogurt cheese, sugar, and vanilla extract. Fold in the fresh fruit. Garnish with kiwi slices and strawberries. Cover and chill until ready to serve.

EACH SERVING PROVIDES
136 calories, 4.6 g protein, 23.8 g carbohydrate
0.5 g fat, 23 mg sodium, 3 mg cholesterol

BLUEBERRY CREAM

YIELD: 4 SERVINGS

Any kind of berry can replace the blueberries in this quick and creamy dessert. A sugar substitute may be added to reduce calorie intake.

1 (16-ounce) package frozen blueberries, thawed (about 2 cups)
1 cup skim milk
2 tablespoons sugar or to taste
2 tablespoons cornstarch mixed with 2 tablespoons skim milk
½ teaspoon pure vanilla extract

Reserve 2 tablespoons of blueberries for the garnish. Process the remainder of the blueberries and strain through a sieve, pressing the pulp with a spoon to force the juice into a bowl. Discard the pulp in the sieve and set aside the bowl of clear, strained berry juice.

In a 3-quart stainless steel saucepan, bring the milk and sugar to a boil on medium-high heat, stirring to prevent sticking. Reduce the heat to low and mix in the blueberry juice. Gradually stir in the cornstarch mixture until the blueberry cream begins to thicken to the consistency of cake batter. Remove saucepan from heat and add vanilla extract. Adjust sugar to taste. Transfer to a dessert bowl and allow to cool. Refrigerate for 2 hours or until set. Sprinkle with reserved blueberries and serve chilled.

EACH SERVING PROVIDES
104 calories, 2.8 g protein, 23.3 g carbohydrate
0.4 g fat, 40 mg sodium, 1 mg cholesterol

BERRY COBBLER

YIELD: 8 SERVINGS

A traditional dessert from down south, this recipe combines fruit with a covering of puffy pastry. Best results are achieved in a toaster oven, because the topping needs to brown quickly; the top rack of the oven should work. Any combination of fresh or frozen sweet berries may be used. Skim milk replaces butter in the dough, which resembles a thick, sticky batter.

2 cups fresh or frozen and thawed
    sweet blueberries
2 cups fresh or frozen and thawed
    sweet strawberries
$\frac{1}{3}$ cup sugar
1 cup all-purpose flour
$2\frac{1}{4}$ teaspoons baking powder
$\frac{3}{4}$ teaspoon cream of tartar
$\frac{1}{4}$ teaspoon salt
$\frac{1}{2}$ cup skim milk

Preheat the oven or toaster oven to 400 degrees F. If frozen berries are used, discard the juice from the thawed berries. If fresh strawberries are used, hull and slice the strawberries. Place the fruit in an 8-inch square baking dish. In a bowl, combine the sugar, flour, baking powder, cream of tartar, and salt. Gradually stir in the milk to make a thick, sticky batter (add as much milk as needed). With a tablespoon, drop the batter over the fruit. Bake uncovered for about 25 minutes or until the topping is puffy and has turned lightly brown. Serve warm or at room temperature, topped with fat-free vanilla yogurt or fat-free ice cream.

EACH SERVING PROVIDES
128 calories, 2.6 g protein, 29.2 g carbohydrate
0.5 g fat, 190 mg sodium, 0 mg cholesterol

"CREAMY" EGGLESS CUSTARD

YIELD: 4 SERVINGS

Top tropical fruit with this lightly spiced custard to complete a satisfying meal. The nutmeg and cinnamon heighten the taste of the custard. If you wish, sugar may be replaced with artificial sweeteners.

2 cups skim milk
2 tablespoons sugar
¼ teaspoon ground cinnamon
¼ teaspoon ground nutmeg
2½ tablespoons cornstarch mixed with
    2 tablespoons cold skim milk
1 teaspoon pure vanilla extract

Combine the milk, sugar, cinnamon, and nutmeg in a 3-quart stainless steel saucepan and bring to a boil on medium-high heat. Stir constantly to prevent milk from sticking. Lower the heat and gradually stir in the cornstarch mixture. Keep stirring until the milk thickens to a custard-like consistency. Remove from the heat and add the vanilla extract. Allow to cool, then transfer to a bowl, cover, and chill. When ready to use, stir to remove the "skin" that forms on the surface.

EACH SERVING PROVIDES
91 calories, 4.5 g protein, 17.2 g carbohydrate
0.3 g fat, 67 mg sodium, 2 mg cholesterol

SERVING SUGGESTION

Serve over fresh tropical or seasonal fruit.

BANANA RAISIN MUFFINS

YIELD: 12 MUFFINS

Muffins made without fat may be more chewy than regular muffins, but they taste just as good. The bananas should be ripe so that they mash easily.

2 ripe bananas, peeled and well mashed
1 cup all-purpose flour
5 tablespoons brown sugar or to taste
1½ teaspoons baking soda
1 teaspoon baking powder
½ cup canned evaporated skim milk
2 tablespoons raisins
½ teaspoon pure vanilla extract

Preheat the oven to 350 degrees F. Line a 12-cup muffin pan with 12 large baking cups. In a bowl, mix all ingredients and stir for about 2 minutes. Pour the batter into the cups two-thirds full. Bake for about 15 minutes. Do not overcook. Muffins should feel just firm to the touch.

EACH MUFFIN PROVIDES
90 calories, 2.1 g protein, 20.5 g carbohydrate
0.2 g fat, 187 mg sodium, 0 mg cholesterol

BLUEBERRY MUFFINS

YIELD: 12 MUFFINS

Ripe fresh blueberries make all the difference in this recipe. Serve warm muffins for breakfast or as a snack.

1 cup all-purpose flour
5 tablespoons brown sugar or to taste
¾ cup canned evaporated skim milk
¾ cup fresh blueberries
1½ teaspoons baking soda
1 teaspoon baking powder
½ teaspoon pure vanilla extract

Preheat the oven to 350 degrees F. Line a 12-cup muffin pan with baking cups. In a bowl, mix all ingredients and stir to form a thick batter. Pour the batter into the baking cups two-thirds full, ensuring that each cup contains some blueberries. Bake for 15 minutes. Serve warm.

EACH MUFFIN PROVIDES
77 calories, 2.2 g protein, 16.6 g carbohydrate
0.2 g fat, 193 mg sodium, 1 mg cholesterol

ALMOST FAT-FREE CHOCOLATE PUDDING

YIELD: 4 SERVINGS

This light recipe is ideal for chocolate lovers. The cocoa does have some fat (1 tablespoon contains about 0.4 grams of saturated fat). The sugar can be replaced with a sweetener, which should be added at the same time as the vanilla extract.

2 cups skim milk
2 tablespoons nonfat dry milk powder
1½ tablespoons unsweetened cocoa
2 tablespoons sugar or to taste
2 heaping tablespoons cornstarch mixed with
    3 tablespoons cold skim milk
¼ teaspoon pure vanilla extract
3 maraschino cherries, drained

Combine the skim milk, milk powder, cocoa, and sugar in a 3-quart stainless steel saucepan. Bring to a boil on high heat, stirring constantly. Lower heat to prevent the mixture from boiling over. Add the cornstarch mixture gradually while stirring at the same time. When the milk thickens to the consistency of cake batter, which happens almost immediately, remove and set aside. (If the milk does not thicken easily, add 1 tablespoon cornstarch mixed with 2 tablespoons cold milk.) Stir in the vanilla extract. Pour the mixture into a fancy serving dish and allow to cool. Refrigerate for at least 3 hours to enable the pudding to set. When the pudding feels firm (test by tipping the bowl gently), garnish with cherries or your favorite fat-free topping. Serve.

EACH SERVING PROVIDES
114 calories, 6.4 g protein, 21.4 g carbohydrate
0.6 g fat, 91 mg sodium, 3 mg cholesterol

SUPERB RICE PUDDING

YIELD: 6 SERVINGS

Ground cardamom gives this delicious dessert a unique flavor. It may be served warm, cold, or at room temperature.

½ cup basmati rice
3 cups skim milk
1 (12-ounce) can evaporated skim milk
3 tablespoons sugar or to taste
2 tablespoons raisins
¼ teaspoon ground cinnamon
¼ teaspoon ground cardamom

Soak the rice in 3 cups of water for 30 minutes and drain. Mix the skim milk, evaporated milk, sugar, raisins, and rice in a 4-quart stainless steel pot and bring to a boil on high heat, stirring continuously to prevent sticking. Cover and cook on very low heat for 30 minutes or until rice is softened and the milk has thickened. Remove from heat. Stir in the cinnamon and cardamom. Pour into a serving bowl and serve warm or cold.

EACH SERVING PROVIDES
178 calories, 10.1 g protein, 33.4 g carbohydrate
0.5 g fat, 138 mg sodium, 5 mg cholesterol

SEMOLINA HALVA

YIELD: 4 SERVINGS

Chopped pistachios, walnuts, and slivered almonds are the traditional topping on this dessert. Our fat-free version may be garnished with raisins and tastes every bit as good!

½ cup semolina
2 tablespoons seedless raisins
2 cups water
½ cup light brown sugar or to taste
¼ teaspoon ground cardamom

Heat a saucepan on medium-high heat. Add the semolina and raisins. Stir constantly and rapidly, about 6 to 8 minutes or until the semolina turns slightly pinkish brown and looks roasted. Do not let it burn. Remove from heat and cool for 5 minutes. Add the water and stir well to remove any lumps. Return to low heat, add sugar and cardamom, and stir well. Cover and cook for about 5 minutes or until water has evaporated. The halva should be the consistency of pumpkin pie filling. Remove from heat and keep covered until ready to serve. It may be served warm or at room temperature.

EACH SERVING PROVIDES
202 calories, 2.9 g protein, 47.3 g carbohydrate
0.3 g fat, 16 mg sodium, 0 mg cholesterol

SENSATIONAL PUDDING

YIELD: 4 SERVINGS

The slender angel hair pasta bears close resemblance to the thin wheat-based noodles that are traditionally used for this dessert. The recipe calls for the dry, shelf-stored pasta. This dessert does thicken as it chills, so care should be taken not to thicken it too much during cooking. Skim milk could be added to achieve the desired consistency if the pudding does get too lumpy. Nuts are the traditional topping (almonds, an optional ingredient due to their high fat content, have been restricted to 4 slivers).

½ cup broken dried angel hair–pasta nests
1½ cups skim milk
2 tablespoons nonfat dry milk powder
2½ tablespoons sugar or to taste
2 tablespoon raisins
1 tablespoon cornstarch mixed with
    3 tablespoons skim milk
⅛ teaspoon ground cardamom
4 slivers of 1 almond, finely chopped

Place the pasta on a cutting board and cover with a piece of foil. Firmly press a rolling pin on the foil and roll back and forth until the pasta is broken up into ¼-inch bits. (The foil prevents the dry pasta from flying around.)

Heat a 3-quart stainless steel saucepan on medium-high heat. Add the pasta bits and stir briskly until the pasta turns a light brown color, 1 to 2 minutes. Remove from heat and cool for a few minutes. Add 2 cups of water to the pasta bits and bring to a boil. Lower the heat and cook the roasted pasta for 6 minutes or until just tender. Drain the pasta and set aside.

Mix the skim milk, milk powder, sugar, and raisins in a 3-quart stainless steel saucepan and bring to a boil on medium heat, stirring continuously. Lower the heat and add the pasta. Gradually stir in the cornstarch mixture and cook until very slightly thickened. Remove from the heat, add the cardamom, and pour into a dessert bowl. Top with almond pieces, chill, and serve.

EACH SERVING PROVIDES
152 calories, 7.0 g protein, 30.2 g carbohydrate
0.6 g fat, 77 mg sodium, 3 mg cholesterol

STRAWBERRY-SEMOLINA WHIP

YIELD: 2 SERVINGS

No meal is complete without a sumptuous dessert. This imaginative dessert is pleasing to the eye and to the palate. The traditional topping would be chopped pecans and walnuts, but since nuts are high in fat, fresh strawberries (in season) are ideal; colorful candied fruit and raisins are also good alternatives.

1 cup skim milk
4 tablespoons semolina
2 tablespoons strawberry jam
2 tablespoons sugar or to taste
½ teaspoon pure vanilla extract
2 to 3 drops red food coloring
Fresh strawberries or raisins

Heat milk on medium heat in a stainless steel saucepan and sprinkle in semolina. Lower the heat and cook for 3 to 4 minutes, stirring constantly until the mixture has the consistency of custard or cake batter. Remove from heat. Stir in the jam and sugar. Set aside to cool. Stir in the vanilla extract and food coloring and mix well until the mixture turns an even, pink color. Turn onto a fancy serving dish and chill. Garnish with fresh strawberries or raisins.

EACH SERVING PROVIDES

223 calories, 7.0 g protein, 47.8 g carbohydrate

0.4 g fat, 65 mg sodium, 2 mg cholesterol

VARIATION

Reduce the strawberry jam to 1 tablespoon and add ½ cup fresh or frozen pureed strawberries. Adjust the sugar to taste (or a sugar substitute can be used to reduce caloric intake; mix it in along with the vanilla and food coloring). Proceed with the rest of the recipe.

VANILLA-STRAWBERRY PARFAIT

YIELD: 6 SERVINGS

This beautiful dessert was an inspiration from a good friend, who was thrilled to learn that I wanted to include it in this book. Serve it in individual stemmed dessert bowls for a fetching effect.

1 package Jell-O Fat-Free Sugar-Free Pudding &
    Pie Filling (vanilla flavor)
18 large fresh strawberries, hulled
2 tablespoons confectioners' sugar
2 ripe bananas, peeled and sliced
½ teaspoon red food coloring
6 medium, whole strawberries

Prepare the pudding according to directions, using skim milk. Set aside to cool, then chill in the refrigerator until set.

Hull 12 strawberries and puree in a food processor with the sugar and bananas. Mix in the food coloring, transfer the puree to a bowl, cover, and chill for at least 1 hour in the refrigerator.

Just before serving, stir the vanilla pudding. Spoon 4 tablespoons of the strawberry-banana puree in each of 6 dessert bowls. Drop 2 tablespoons of vanilla pudding over the puree, and garnish each dessert bowl with a whole strawberry. Serve cold.

EACH SERVING PROVIDES

99 calories, 3.5 g protein, 21.7 g carbohydrate

0.5 g fat, 43 mg sodium, 1 mg cholesterol

STRAWBERRIES 'N CREAM

This dessert is ideal when fresh sweet strawberries are in season, but frozen strawberries may also be substituted. The "cream" could be made a day in advance, then covered and chilled in the refrigerator.

2 cups fresh or frozen strawberries
1 heaping tablespoon all-purpose flour
1 cup skim milk
1 tablespoon nonfat dry milk powder
1½ tablespoons sugar
¼ teaspoon pure vanilla extract

Wash and reserve 4 strawberries for garnish. Wash, hull and slice in halves or thirds (depending on the size) the rest of the fresh strawberries, or thaw the frozen strawberries.

Heat a 3-quart stainless steel saucepan on medium-high heat. Add the flour and stir briskly until the flour is toasted to a light almond color; this will take no more than 1 minute. Remove pan from heat and set aside to cool for a few minutes. Gradually add the milk (stirring to avoid lumps), milk powder, and

Desserts

••••

278

sugar. If lumps do form, blend or process the cooled mixture in a food processor. Stir the mixture constantly over medium heat until it thickens to a creamy consistency. Remove from heat, add the vanilla extract, allow to cool, and then chill. Arrange the strawberries in individual serving dishes or a large dessert bowl. Pour the "cream" over the fruit and garnish with the fresh reserved strawberries.

EACH SERVING PROVIDES
75 calories, 3.4 g protein, 15.2 g carbohydrate
0.4 g fat, 42 mg sodium, 1 mg cholesterol

VANILLA-FLAVORED YOGURT

YIELD: 6 SERVINGS

Once you have mastered the art of making plain yogurt, this recipe should be easy.

3 cups skim milk
1 cup nonfat dry milk powder
2 tablespoons brown sugar or to taste
½ teaspoon pure vanilla extract
2 tablespoons nonfat plain yogurt with active
    yogurt cultures (page 249)

In a 3-quart stainless steel saucepan, mix the skim milk and milk powder and bring to a boil on medium-high heat, stirring constantly to ensure it does not stick or boil over. Remove from heat and add the brown sugar. Return the milk to low heat and stir. Let the milk "roll" or simmer for 1 minute, stirring constantly. Remove from heat. Stir in the vanilla extract. Pour into a glass bowl and set aside, uncovered, to cool to about 110 degrees F. Test by feeling the milk with a clean finger. It should feel comfortably warm to the touch, about the temperature of bath water.

In a small bowl, stir the yogurt with a spoon until smooth. When the milk is fairly warm, stir in the yogurt. Promptly cover the bowl and set aside in a warm place, away from the draft, to set. A shawl or warm blanket wrapped around the bowl aids in keeping the milk mixture warm and helps in the yogurt process.

After about 4 hours, uncover the bowl and slightly tilt it. The yogurt should have set like pudding. If not, cover, wrap, and let stand another hour in a warm place. Refrigerate immediately after it has set. Serve chilled.

EACH SERVING PROVIDES
138 calories, 11.7 g protein, 21.4 g carbohydrate
0.2 g fat, 176 mg sodium, 6 mg cholesterol

INDEX

Index

****

Index

••••

Index

....